John R. Mott, the American YMCA, and Revolutionary Russia

AMERICANS IN REVOLUTIONARY RUSSIA

Vol. 1
Albert Rhys Williams, *Through the Russian Revolution*, edited by
William Benton Whisenhunt (2016)

Vol. 2
Princess Julia Cantacuzène, Countess Spéransky, née Grant, *Russian People: Revolutionary Recollections*, edited by Norman E. Saul (2016)

Vol. 3
Ernest Poole, *The Village: Russian Impressions*, edited by Norman E. Saul (2017)

Vol. 4
John Reed, *Ten Days That Shook the World*, edited by
William Benton Whisenhunt (2017)

Vol. 5
Louise Bryant, *Six Red Months in Russia*, edited by Lee A. Farrow (2017)

Vol. 6
Edward Alsworth Ross, *Russia in Upheaval*, edited by Rex A. Wade (2017)

Vol. 7
Donald Thompson, *Donald Thompson in Russia*, edited by David H. Mould (2017)

Vol. 8
Arthur Bullard, *The Russian Pendulum: Autocracy—Democracy—Bolshevism*, edited by
David W. McFadden (2019)

Vol. 9
David Francis, *Russia from the American Embassy*,
edited by Vladimir V. Noskov (2019)

Vol. 10
Pauline S. Crosley, *Intimate Letters from Petrograd*, edited by Lee A. Farrow (2019)

Vol. 11
Madeleine Z. Doty, *"The Bolshevik Revolution Had Descended on Me": Madeleine Z. Doty's Russian Revolution*, edited by Julia L. Mickenberg (2019)

Vol. 12
John R. Mott, the American YMCA, and Revolutionary Russia, edited by Matthew Lee Miller (2020)

Vol. 13
Carl W. Ackerman, *Trailing the Bolsheviki: Twelve Thousand Miles with the Allies in Siberia*, edited by Ivan Kurilla (2020)

Vol. 14
Charles Edward Russell, *Unchained Russia*, edited by Rex A. Wade (2021)

Series General Editors:
Norman E. Saul and William Benton Whisenhunt

John R. Mott, the American YMCA, and Revolutionary Russia

Excerpts From Recent Experiences and Impressions in Russia by
John R. Mott

and
Service with Fighting Men

Edited and Introduction by
Matthew Lee Miller

ANTHEM PRESS

Anthem Press
An imprint of Wimbledon Publishing Company
www.anthempress.com

First published by Slavica Publishers, Indiana University, USA, 2020

This edition first published in UK and USA 2026
by ANTHEM PRESS
75–76 Blackfriars Road, London SE1 8HA, UK
or PO Box 9779, London SW19 7ZG, UK
and
244 Madison Ave #116, New York, NY 10016, USA

Copyright © 2026 Matthew Lee Miller editorial matter and selection;
individual chapters © individual contributors

The moral right of the authors has been asserted.

All rights reserved. Without limiting the rights under copyright reserved above,
no part of this publication may be reproduced, stored or introduced into
a retrieval system, or transmitted, in any form or by any means
(electronic, mechanical, photocopying, recording or otherwise),
without the prior written permission of both the copyright
owner and the above publisher of this book.

British Library Cataloguing-in-Publication Data
A catalogue record for this book is available from the British Library.

Library of Congress Cataloging-in-Publication Data: Submitted

ISBN-13: 978-1-83999-736-5 (Hbk)
ISBN-10: 1-83999-736-2 (Hbk)

ISBN-13: 978-1-83999-737-2 (Pbk)
ISBN-10: 1-83999-737-0 (Pbk)

Cover design: Tracey Theriault

This title is also available as an eBook.

CONTENTS

Editor's Introduction   xi
    Matthew Lee Miller

Editor's Note   xxv

Acknowledgments   xxvii

JOHN R. MOTT, THE AMERICAN YMCA, AND REVOLUTIONARY RUSSIA

Part 1

EXCERPTS FROM
RECENT EXPERIENCES AND IMPRESSIONS IN RUSSIA: EXTRACTS FROM CORRESPONDENCE AND ADDRESSES OF JOHN R. MOTT, MEMBER OF THE SPECIAL DIPLOMATIC MISSION OF THE UNITED STATES TO RUSSIA, MAY–AUGUST, 1917

I. Letter From John R. Mott Regarding a Most Urgent Need in Russia   3

II. Speech by John R. Mott at a Dinner Given by Mr. Emanuel Nobel at His Home in Petrograd, June 21, 1917   8

III. Letter from Major-General H. L. Scott to John R. Mott   12

IV. Letter from John R. Mott Regarding Recent Religious Developments in Russia   14

V. Address of John R. Mott, at the Great Sobor of the
Russian Orthodox Church, Moscow, June 19, 1917   25

VI. Letter from the High Procurator of the
Russian Orthodox Church to John R. Mott   30

Part 2

EXCERPTS FROM
SERVICE WITH FIGHTING MEN: AN ACCOUNT OF
THE WORK OF THE AMERICAN
YOUNG MEN'S CHRISTIAN ASSOCIATIONS IN THE WORLD WAR,
VOLUME 2

I. Chapter XLVIII, Russia   35

II. Chapter LVIII, Wartime Activities in Russia   48

Index   85

ILLUSTRATIONS

Cyrus H. McCormick, Jr., and John R. Mott   Figure 1

Root Mission to Russia   Figure 2

The American Mission to Russia   Figure 3

Summer 1917   Figure 4

Members of the American Mission to Russia and the
Board of Trade of Petrograd   Figure 5

EDITOR'S INTRODUCTION
Matthew Lee Miller

John R. Mott's *Recent Experiences and Impressions in Russia* presents a collection of public addresses and letters created during his participation in a United States diplomatic mission to Russia—sent by President Woodrow Wilson and led by Elihu Root—from May to August 1917. These historical documents (printed in 1917 but never published) describe this Root Mission and offer perspectives on several momentous events and leaders of the era: World War I, the February Revolution, members of the Provisional Government, and leaders of the Russian Orthodox Church. The documents include a proposal for the Young Men's Christian Association (YMCA) to carry out a program of service among Russia's military. *Service with Fighting Men: An Account of the Work of the American Young Men's Christian Associations in the World War* (published in 1924) presents the YMCA's official description and evaluation of the work carried out in Russia in response to Mott's plans.[1]

In order to provide context to the reader, this introduction provides key information on the work of the American YMCA in Russia, the role of Mott as a leader for this organization, and a survey of the association's work with soldiers during this time.[2] The goal of this introduction is to encourage analysis of the texts (keeping in mind that the events of November 1917 had not yet taken place by the time the first set of documents were written). Mott wrote with optimism, idealism, and self-confidence—but, of course, he did not know the future. The second set of documents demonstrates how quickly events in Russia shifted in this era.

The YMCA began its service among Russian workers and students in 1900. The *Mayak* (Lighthouse) program in St. Petersburg offered a wide range of athletic, social,

---

[1] William Howard Taft, et al., eds., *Service with Fighting Men: An Account of the Work of the American Young Men's Christian Associations in the World War*, vol. 2 (New York: Association Press, 1924), 270–82, 419–57.

[2] This introduction includes updated and revised material from the editor's *The American YMCA and Russian Culture: The Preservation and Expansion of Orthodox Christianity, 1900–1940* (Lanham, MD: Lexington Books, 2013); and "The American YMCA and Russian Politics: Critics and Supporters of Socialism, 1900–1940," in *New Perspectives on Russian-American Relations*, ed. William Benton Whisenhunt and Norman E. Saul (New York: Routledge, 2015), 161–77.

educational, and religious opportunities for young men. These programs reflected those offered in the United Kingdom, the United States, and around the world since the middle of the nineteenth century. Following the outbreak of the First World War, many "Y" workers expanded these services in Russia to provide humanitarian assistance to soldiers and prisoners of war. These efforts were requested by the US and Russian governments. They set up libraries, promoted athletic competitions, and organized concerts and classes for men in uniform. During the war, the YMCA staff members, known as "secretaries," formed the largest group of Americans living in Russia.

However, the revolutionary changes of 1917 sharply increased the political tensions experienced by the association. The links of this nongovernmental organization to the US government contributed to the closure of the association on Soviet territory. After the war, Y workers continued to serve among émigrés in creative ways. They supported the development of the Russian Student Christian Movement, which brought together many young Russians from across Europe. In Paris, the YMCA supported the Orthodox Theological Institute, later named the St. Sergius Theological Academy. This was the only Russian Orthodox educational program of its kind at that time. The most well-known contribution was the YMCA Press, which published a remarkable variety of literary, philosophical, and spiritual books in Russian. The YMCA's service among Russians is a fascinating example of Russian-American cultural relations.

This introduction presents the YMCA's work with Russian, Allied, and Central Power soldiers within the territory of Russia from 1914 to 1919. First, it looks at the needs which the association detected and the purposes established by the leaders. It examines key developments and explores the program's finances. Then, it looks at a few controversial issues and attempts to evaluate the Y's wartime programs in Russia, which leads to the primary point: the YMCA faced a complex challenge in conducting a global program of philanthropy, which was made possible by the support of the US government. YMCA staff members filled controversial public roles as Americans in Russia during a politically volatile period of world war and revolution.

Mott's convictions on the reasons why the American YMCA should serve soldiers in Russia developed well before 1917. All in all, more than six million soldiers and civilians were held in prison camps across Europe during the war. Russia held 1.5 million inside its borders, while 2.5 million Russians were held as prisoners of war or were missing in foreign countries. These numbers far exceeded the number expected by the participating countries and the resources available to provide the required services. The Hague Conventions of 1899 and 1907 defined the responsibilities for governments holding captives during a war. Those held must receive "food, quarters, and clothing, on the same footing as the troops of the Government which has captured them." The unexpectedly high number of captives forced the nations involved to find solutions—including the participation of neutral nations. By May

1915, the United States government emerged as the only body which was capable of providing aid to these prisoners. During the first months of the war, the US policy of neutrality was interpreted to exclude any involvement with POWs. However, appeals from Europe and political influence within the US led to a revision of this position. The Department of State agreed to provide relief services for prisoners under the direction of the American Consular Service. Along with other neutral nations, US representatives would inspect prison camps, supervise the provision of supplies, and distribute financial aid to prisoners. However, American embassies in Europe lacked the personnel, infrastructure, and experience required to carry out this large-scale commitment: "The American diplomatic corps had no experience providing social welfare assistance to foreign nationals." The Wilson administration soon realized that nongovernmental organizations must participate in the program if the United States was to fulfill its agreements. The American YMCA responded to the request of the government to provide physical, mental, and spiritual assistance for war prisoners. The YMCA launched the international War Prisoners Aid program to assist POWs of any nationality or religious belief. The American program functioned under the World's Alliance of YMCAs (based in neutral Geneva, Switzerland) and worked with other national associations.[3]

John R. Mott was the primary catalyst for the expansion of the YMCA's work with soldiers across Europe, and specifically in Russia. Mott grew up in Postville, Iowa, in a Methodist home. He joined the YMCA student ministry during his years at Cornell University. After graduating from Cornell in 1888, he embarked on a career with the YMCA. Initially he served as a recruiter of students, but by 1890, he became the director of the YMCA's college and university ministry. In 1895, he coordinated the founding of the World Student Christian Federation. This organization attempted to support and unite student Christian movements throughout the world. For this and other cooperative Christian ventures, Mott later received the Nobel Peace Prize in 1946.

Mott deeply influenced the Russian ministry of the YMCA. Although he participated in this work only intermittently, Mott contributed to the ministry throughout the first half of the twentieth century. His direct involvement began in 1899

---

[3] Kenneth Andrew Steuer, "Pursuit of an 'Unparalleled Opportunity': The American Young Men's Christian Association and Prisoner-of-War Diplomacy Among the Central Power Nations during World War I, 1914–1923" (PhD diss., University of Minnesota, 1997), 1–4; and Paul B. Anderson to Eugene P. Trani, March 29, 1973, attachment to letter 1, 1966–84, Biographical Records, Paul B. Anderson, Kautz Family YMCA Archives [hereafter KFYA], University of Minnesota Libraries, Minneapolis. A general source is the archival document "Meeting of the War Historical Bureau of the Young Men's Christian Association," April 1, 1920, KFYA, Russian Work Restricted, Correspondence and Reports, 1918–1921, Correspondence and Reports, 1920. See also Paul B. Anderson, "Russian Prisoners of War" [no date], Paul B. Anderson Papers, University of Illinois at Urbana-Champaign Archives [hereafter PBAP].

when he encouraged the founding of the Russian Student Christian Movement, and in the following years, he provided guidance and financial support for the ministry. However, Mott contributed most significantly through his indirect influence, for several of his priorities provided guidelines for the direction of the YMCA's ministry in Russia: coordinating world evangelization, encouraging ministry cooperation, motivating indigenous leadership, supporting Russian Orthodoxy, and providing leadership training.

Mott traveled with a group to Europe in September 1914 to inspect the situation and determine the possibilities of YMCA assistance. They witnessed overcrowded hospitals and the difficulties in communication between wounded soldiers and family members. Mott and other YMCA leaders were motivated to help and to visit those in prison, as taught in the gospel of Matthew. He decided to raise millions of dollars and recruit secretaries to address the needs they observed. He met with the International Committee of the YMCA in December 1914 and described the tragic impact of the war on soldiers and refugees. Mott recognized that the war was a disaster, but he expressed his usual optimism. He suggested that the war was an opportunity to serve an enormous number of people across Europe. The main issue was how to provide relief and maintain American neutrality.[4] Mott met with President Woodrow Wilson at the White House in January 1915 to discuss his experiences in Europe. The two had met at Wesleyan University in Connecticut in 1889. Wilson had been a professor at the school, and Mott had been visiting as a representative of the Student Volunteer Movement. This YMCA-supported movement facilitated the service of US college graduates in Christian ministries around the world. Another example of the connection had been Wilson's offer to Mott of an honorary degree from Princeton in 1910. Mott and Wilson shared a similar optimistic Protestant worldview. At the 1915 meeting, they spoke about ways to develop YMCA service to POWs and maintain US neutrality. They agreed on a plan that would "extend relief to war prisoners in both Allied and Central Power countries" and "would meet a desperate need…. The American YMCA now had the President's support for an ambitious relief program in Europe."[5]

The association and the US government became increasingly interdependent: each side relied on the other to fulfill goals. YMCA secretaries counted on American ambassadors in Berlin, Paris, Rome, Vienna, and Petrograd to make successful contact with local officials. "The Association's standing was clearly bolstered by official American support." Wilson's diplomats provided channels of communication and political information to the YMCA as well. The Y provided a variety of specific aid for US diplomatic officials, who were overloaded with a number of international obligations. Secretaries submitted needed reports on POW camp locations and

---

[4] Steuer, "Pursuit of an 'Unparalleled Opportunity,'" 45–47.

[5] Ibid., 48–50.

conditions—freeing officials from this responsibility. The YMCA also assisted the US government by distributing food and medical supplies to POWs. However, this was not the primary responsibility of the association. President Wilson's approach could be described as corporatism—achieving government goals by utilizing large nongovernmental organizations.[6]

The YMCA began working with soldiers in Russia in 1915. In June of that year, YMCA secretaries Archibald Harte and George Day visited several POW camps in Russia to gain information on conditions and opportunities. They were authorized by Russian General Mikhail Alekseevich Beliaev. Early in their trip, they met with the mayor of Moscow and shared about the YMCA's work with Russian prisoners in Germany. They visited POW camps and a hospital—where leaders requested books and athletic equipment. They examined facilities across Russia—including Omsk and Tomsk in Siberia. They reported good conditions, but the need for equipment for recreation.[7] YMCA staffer Donald A. Lowrie soon began to work with POWs at a camp in Tomsk; he organized classes into twenty-three subjects, including French, commerce and trade, aeronautics, and geology. They also organized a library and weekly religious services for Protestants, Catholics, and Jews.[8]

YMCA secretary Jerome Davis led the first steps in work with Russian soldiers—in addition to POWs. In January 1917, Russian General Aleksei Nikolaevich Kuropatkin allowed the Y to work with one regiment in Turkestan in Central Asia. In February, the Y was permitted to work with all Russian troops in Turkestan. In July, the work expanded to the six regiments in Moscow. In August, the prime minister approved the YMCA to work with troops in Irkutsk, Tomsk, Kazan, Kiev, and Odessa—but Y secretaries were not allowed to work at the front. In September, the minister of war gave an official endorsement to the YMCA, and the prime minister allowed the Y to work on all fronts. This led to an accelerated deployment of Y secretaries and supplies throughout the country. The government provided a building in Moscow for the Y, and a general authorized forty buildings on the Western Front. A Moscow YMCA city council was formed, which included the mayor of Moscow, the minister of justice, the American consul, and other officials. A national YMCA office was organized in Moscow. Davis described the main goal of the wartime work to US readers in this way: "The central aim of the Association's War Work is to serve Russia, her government and her soldiers with all the power at our command. We believe that our

---

[6] Ibid., 447–49.

[7] A. C. Harte, "Harte and Day to the Hospitals and German Prisoners' Camps in Siberia, Petrograd, June 25, 1915," KFYA, Russian Work Restricted, Correspondence and Reports, 1903–1917, Correspondence and Reports, 1915–1916, 1–4.

[8] Donald A. Lowrie to John R. Mott, September 11 (24), 1916, KFYA, Russian Work Restricted, Correspondence and Reports, 1903–1917, Correspondence and Reports, 1915–1916, 1–2.

message will be carried not through our words but through our deeds. We feel that the closer we live up to the ideals of the Master in service the more we will demonstrate the ideal for which the Association stands." Davis went on to explain, "During the two weeks that the soldier is back from the trenches there is little or nothing for him to do.... His main occupation is smoking ... sleeping or engaging in gambling or other harmful amusements." YMCA leaders provided supplies and organization for reading, writing, games, and music.[9]

Mott served as the catalyst for YMCA expansion of work among soldiers, but the implementation of his plans in Russia was carried out by a series of leaders. Archibald Harte supervised the War Prisoners' Aid in Russia and other countries in Europe—and he was originally responsible for the Russian army work. He left Russia in the summer of 1917, delegating his authority to acting senior secretary Jerome Davis. Harte planned to return in October 1917, but he was not able to do so. Davis was criticized for weak administrative skills, so Y secretaries formed a War Work Council in November 1917. His successor, Ethan Colton, was appointed in December 1917, but he was not able to arrive in Russia until March 1918. Therefore, as one YMCA report explained, "During this entire critical period the administration was in the hands of men whose tenure of office was temporary and who did not feel themselves in a position to make decisions of the most vital importance."[10] When new YMCA recruits arrived in Russia, they were often frustrated by a lack of organization and direction.

The service of the American YMCA among soldiers shifted significantly as it adjusted to Russia's dramatic political changes. Over three hundred Americans gathered together for this service and worked among many levels of Russian society in many regions.[11] This included all YMCA workers with prisoners, soldiers, and civilians during the war. The work can be examined in three periods. The first period stretched from June 1915 to March 1918. This period included the abdication of Emperor Nicholas II and the Bolshevik Revolution. It ended with the Treaty of Brest-Litovsk, ending Russia's participation in the war. The second period, March 1918 to August 1918, was a transitional one, which included the rise of the Soviet

---

[9] Jerome Davis, "Association History in the Making in Russia," October 22 (November 4), 1917, KFYA, Russian Work Restricted, Correspondence and Reports, 1903–1917, Correspondence and Reports, 1917, 1–2.

[10] Taft, et al., *Service with Fighting Men*, 427; Donald E. Davis and Eugene P. Trani, "The American YMCA and the Russian Revolution," *Slavic Review* 33, no. 3 (1974): 475.

[11] Memorandum from Crawford Wheeler to John R. Mott and E. T. Colton, "Report on War time Activities in Russia," November 22, 1919, KFYA, Russia, Colton E. T., Reports, Addresses, and Papers, WWI Field Reports, binder 2, 3–5.

government. The third period, from August 1918 until 1919, included the Russian Civil War[12] and Allied intervention in Russia.

The focus of the first period was the Russian army. The United States declared war on Germany in April 1917, so this ended the US position of neutrality. This necessitated the withdrawal of American secretaries working with Russian POWs in several camps in Germany and Austria-Hungary. In June 1917, the United States recognized the Provisional Government, which had been set up after the abdication of Emperor Nicholas II on March 15, 1917. This led to the formation of a diplomatic mission to Russia from the US government, led by Elihu Root, which included Mott. The Root Mission attempted to evaluate how to assist the new Provisional Government and to encourage continued Russian participation in the war. While in Petrograd, Mott initiated a variety of discussions with many influential Orthodox leaders.[13] Mott supported the Russian Orthodox Church as the primary spiritual expression of the Russian people. He had accepted a negative evaluation of the church during his years at Cornell, but rejected this evaluation after extensive contact with Eastern Christians. Over the years he established a network of friendships within the worldwide community and frequently expressed his admiration of the church. Mott emphasized that the YMCA supported the Orthodox community due to its doctrinal foundations, rich liturgy, and perseverance. On this trip, Mott secured permission to expand welfare work with Russian troops, so he began to personally recruit workers after his return to the US. He recruited college students and graduates who had experience with YMCA programs in the US. In October 1917, just before the Bolshevik uprising, the Provisional Government unanimously adopted a resolution which formally approved the work of the YMCA among troops of the Russian army. This approval granted railroad transportation, customs clearance, and postal delivery to the association at no charge.[14] Approximately fifty new YMCA recruits arrived soon after the October Revolution. They soon learned that the new Soviet government planned to negotiate a peace settlement. Russian soldiers were leaving the front, and it became impossible to continue formal work with the troops.[15] Soon after the October Revolution, YMCA work with Russian soldiers ended at the fronts. By March 1918, all work with the Russian army dissolved. The Soviet government signed the Brest-Litovsk peace treaty with Germany on March 3, 1918. The YMCA soon adjusted its goals, programs, and policies for the new situation at a conference in the Russian city of Samara in March 1918. Many secretaries ended their YMCA

---

[12] Ibid., 7–9.

[13] See John W. Long and C. Howard Hopkins, "The Church and the Russian Revolution: Conversations of John R. Mott with Orthodox Church Leaders, June–July 1917," *St. Vladimir's Theological Quarterly* 20, no. 3 (1976): 161–80.

[14] Taft, et al., *Service with Fighting Men*, 428–29.

[15] Ibid., 419.

service, but others adopted new responsibilities serving Russian civilians and returning prisoners of war.[16]

The second period of YMCA work with soldiers continued from March to August 1918. New civilian programs were organized in central Russian cities, and a YMCA agricultural exhibition traveled along the Volga River.[17] Limited work with Russian soldiers continued.

The third period began in August 1918 and included the Russian Civil War. At this time, Allied forces, including American troops, were deployed to Murmansk and Archangelsk on the Arctic coastline, as well as Vladivostok on the Pacific. This intervention during the Russian Civil War was part of the Allied strategy for the World War. US troops were sent to Archangelsk and Vladivostok to prevent German seizure of Allied military equipment. However, what began as a pragmatic military operation evolved into an indecisive struggle against the Bolsheviks. Allied troops gave "half-hearted" support to White armies opposing the Red Army. For Soviet leaders and historians, this intervention functioned for many years as key evidence of a Western plan to strangle Soviet Russia.[18] The participation of the YMCA in the Allied intervention was one of the most controversial aspects of the association's work. US military intervention led to the end of YMCA work in territory controlled by the Soviet government. Intervention required the evacuation of the American embassy and all official representatives of the US from Soviet Russia. The US government could provide no protection, so virtually all Y staff members left Soviet-controlled territory. Therefore, the new focus of work became various Allied units and Russian civilians in northern Russia and Siberia.[19]

The YMCA served a variety of people during this period in areas not controlled by the Soviet government. The YMCA program of service to Allied soldiers began in Archangelsk during the first half of 1918. Approximately five thousand American troops arrived in the fall, and twenty-five American secretaries came in October. YMCA secretaries followed the deployment of the troops. Eventually, YMCA personnel included nearly a hundred American, Canadian, and British secretaries, plus Russian assistants. Four American Y secretaries were captured while working near the front with Allied soldiers. Two were released in Moscow with the help of the YMCA representative in Copenhagen, who traveled into the country to negotiate their release. In August 1919, the US embassy instructed all Americans to withdraw, so the American YMCA program ended. The American Y men left northern Russia by September 1919. The association operated work for Allied troops in the Russian

---

[16] Ibid., 427, 430–31.

[17] Wheeler, "Report on War time Activities in Russia," 8.

[18] Robert C. Grogin, *Natural Enemies: The United States and the Soviet Union in the Cold War, 1917–1991* (Lanham, MD: Lexington Books, 2001), 16–17.

[19] Taft, et al., *Service with Fighting Men*, 420, 433–35.

Far East and Siberia as well. By February 1919, five association huts were operating for Allied soldiers near Vladivostok. The program ended with the Soviet advances in fall 1919.[20]

Individual American YMCA staff members experienced their service in Russia in a wide variety of ways. As mentioned earlier, Jerome Davis was one of the first American YMCA secretaries to work with soldiers in Russia. He was recruited personally by John R. Mott, who spoke with him at Oberlin College. Davis did not want to interrupt his studies, but Mott told him, "The instruments of destruction in war today are so terrible that the war cannot last more than a few months." Davis began his work with little knowledge of Russian, so he studied on the ship while crossing the Atlantic. Soon after his arrival, he made a seven-day train trip to Turkestan to begin working with POWs. This quick initiation into work seemed to be motivated by the YMCA agreement made with German authorities. They agreed to allow Y men to assist Allied prisoners if the YMCA served the German, Austrian, and Turkish prisoners in Russia. Davis later went to the capital city and met with Alexander Kerensky for negotiations on the YMCA's work. Davis was in Moscow during the Bolshevik takeover in 1917, along with a number of other secretaries. He then took the train to Petrograd to obtain permission from the new Soviet government to continue the YMCA's work with soldiers. The work was welcomed by a Soviet official who provided a note authorizing the withdrawal of YMCA funds from the state bank. However, the bank cashier refused to provide the funds and demanded a letter from either Leon Trotsky or Vladimir Lenin. Davis then managed to meet with Trotsky and explain the YMCA's work. Trotsky provided a note for the bank, and Davis had no more problems. Later, Davis was strongly opposed to US intervention: "I was astounded to learn that the United States was planning to help overthrow the Bolshevik regime." He agreed to begin working in Archangelsk only if the Bolshevik regime collapsed in two months, as predicted by the US ambassador. However, this diplomat's prediction proved to be inaccurate, so Davis departed.[21]

Davis's opposition to the US government's actions stood in sharp contrast to the views of Mott, who strongly supported President Wilson and his political philosophy. Mott supported US entry into the war and opposed the Bolshevik regime. His Christian vision became closely tied to America's political agendas and national ambitions. Ironically, his identification with US government interests contributed to the continuing ban on the YMCA's work in the USSR.[22]

---

[20] Ibid., 435–37, 441, 445; G. S. Phelps, "Siberian Expedition Report," November 3, 1920, KFYA, Siberia, Russian Work Restricted, North Russia: Archangel, Murmansk, Siberia, 38.

[21] Jerome Davis, *A Life Adventure for Peace: An Autobiography* (New York: Citadel, 1967), 24–26, 43–49.

[22] M. Craig Barnes, "John R. Mott: A Conversionist in a Pluralist World" (PhD diss., University of Chicago, 1992), 222–24.

Paul B. Anderson, a key secretary for outreach to soldiers, worked to serve the Russian people from his first trip in 1917 until his death in 1985. He had a long-term, in-depth involvement with Russian life and made a serious attempt to understand its language, history, and culture. He provided leadership or support for almost every aspect of the YMCA's Russian ministry. He grew up in Madrid, Iowa, and studied at the University of Iowa. In 1917, he was invited to serve as personal assistant to John R. Mott for the US diplomatic Root Mission to Russia. Mott, the leader of the American YMCA's global ministry, served as a mentor to Anderson throughout his life. Anderson arrived in Petrograd on June 12, 1917, and remained in the city after the Root Mission returned to America. Initially, he focused on assisting with the administration of YMCA service to prisoners of war. The Bolshevik uprising in 1917 disrupted the work, yet Anderson continued with his duties until September 1918, when he was arrested in Moscow. Suspected of "counter-revolutionary" activity, he was taken by a government security officer to the Lubianka prison. He was released, but shortly thereafter the YMCA ended its full-scale service in Soviet Russia. From 1920 to 1924, Anderson lived in Berlin and participated in a variety of creative service programs. During these years in Berlin and then in Paris, Anderson's understanding of Russian culture grew. He emerged as one of the first Western experts on religion in the Soviet Union.

The YMCA's service to soldiers and prisoners of war was initially funded by several wealthy philanthropists in response to Mott's requests. However, rising costs led to a broader fundraising approach. The YMCA worked with several other American international social welfare organizations in promoting the United War Work Campaign. This campaign eventually gathered 203 million dollars, the largest amount gathered for a voluntary program on record. The share for the American YMCA amounted to nearly sixty percent—over 100 million dollars.[23] The American Y spent nearly eight million dollars for wartime work in Russia.[24]

YMCA leaders viewed the rise of socialism and the Bolshevik Revolution with a diversity of perspectives. As leaders of a prominent international program of philanthropy, the work and relationships of secretaries brought them into direct contact with Emperor Nicholas II, Vladimir Lenin, and Leon Trotsky. They also met a wide variety of workers, peasants, and soldiers. YMCA secretaries were reflective writers in their reports and letters about their experiences. Some condemned the political changes, a few championed the revolution, but most expressed ambivalence as they watched chaos unfold and stretch into civil war. None were monarchists, and none were communists, but the YMCA staff included secretaries holding political

---

[23] Steuer, "Pursuit of an 'Unparalleled Opportunity,'" 456.

[24] Taft, et al., *Service with Fighting Men*, 456 [no details provided with these statistics]; "Recapitulation of Budget for Russian Army Work," KFYA, Russian Work Restricted, Correspondence and Reports, 1918–1921, Correspondence and Reports, 1919.

views from right to center to left. The February Revolution was welcomed by the majority, but most Y men responded with uncertainty to the October Revolution, since they did not understand even the basics of the Bolsheviks' approach. Eventually, the clear majority of secretaries expressed a negative view about the October events. The two primary leaders of all YMCA service among Russians were John R. Mott and Paul B. Anderson. These men attempted to understand Marxism and concluded that it was fundamentally alien to Russian culture. They did not use liberal democracy as an exclusive standard for political ideology, but they argued that Russian Marxists should respect a diversity of political opinion. Mott and Anderson were very influential within the YMCA's Russian program and voiced the majority opinion against socialism.

Three staff members, Jerome Davis, Sherwood Eddy, and Julius Hecker, emphasized the visions of Russian socialists. They encouraged their American readers to consider the progress made by these radicals in bringing justice to oppressed workers and peasants. These views were based on their own dissatisfaction with Western democracy and traditional Protestant religion. This vocal minority of the YMCA's Russian work staff was sympathetic to many aspects of the Bolsheviks' program. They did not support the use of violence or the Soviet stance on atheism. However, they envisioned a future peaceful, socialist Russia with a philosophy which combined Marxist and Christian aspects.

The YMCA faced a complex challenge in conducting a global program of philanthropy, which was made possible by the support of the US government. YMCA staff members filled controversial public roles as Americans in Russia during a politically volatile period of world war and revolution. Most steered clear of any political action. However, the variety of political opinions and agendas held by YMCA representatives demonstrates that the Y was not a government tool with a program dictated by Washington.

The YMCA's work with soldiers raised heated controversies. After the October Revolution, a variety of critics from all sides in the US and Russia denounced the Y for several reasons. Soviet leaders suspected that secretaries were meddling Allied supporters, but they accepted material aid for Russians returning from POW camps. Opponents of the Bolsheviks often assumed that they were Marxist sympathizers. The Bolsheviks saw the Y as a tool of Washington, since the Y frequently assisted their enemies—especially in North Russia and Siberia.[25] The Y faced a difficult dilemma: it attempted to support the Allied cause *and* also support any troops that needed assistance. The concluding YMCA report summarized, "This very non-partisanship made all partisans suspicious."[26] In the US, Mott's wartime alignment of American

---

[25] Davis and Trani, "The American YMCA and the Russian Revolution," 479, 483.

[26] Taft, et al., *Service with Fighting Men*, 420.

and Christian goals was popular with many mainline Protestants. Other Christian groups rejected his approach.[27]

In spite of the widespread YMCA optimism, World War I undermined the YMCA's worldwide advance rather than expanding its influence. Before the war, the American, British, and German associations worked closely as partners in the World Alliance of YMCAs. The war broke the cohesion of this arrangement. Members of the alliance did not come together for a meeting between 1914 and 1920.[28] In addition, the global Protestant movement was weakened by the close connection between the churches and the war effort. As one scholar explained, "The identification of the missionary and national causes in wartime led to a serious loss of credibility for missions in the decade after the war." The American entry into the war reflected the experience of many European nations with an enthusiasm for a holy war. Most Protestant, Catholic, and Jewish leaders supported the war effort. The opposition of Quakers and Mennonites was not politely received.[29]

Evaluating the YMCA's service among soldiers is not a simple task. In spite of these suspicions and many limitations, the YMCA significantly improved prisoner conditions in the locations where it was able to operate. The results of the YMCA POW relief program may have matched the goals in quality, but not in quantity. The secretaries simply could not serve the vast number of prisoners, and made contact with only a small percentage of them. As mentioned earlier, Russia held 1.5 million inside its borders; 2.5 million Russians were held as prisoners of war or missing in foreign countries. One historian summarized, "The suffering of the POW in the Great War may have been too great a challenge, especially for just one social welfare organization."[30] The YMCA's own evaluations of this work in Russia express ambivalence and identify both failures and successes. In conclusion, the American YMCA's attempts to serve soldiers raised more controversy from more critics than any other aspect of the Russian service. This criticism should be evaluated in light of the wider long-term goal of the organization to provide religious, physical, and social support to all groups of Russian youth.

---

[27] See clipping from "The Gospel Message," published by the Gospel Union Publishing Company, Kansas City, MO, KFYA, Russian Work Restricted, Correspondence and Reports, 1903–1917, Correspondence and Reports, 1915–1916, 11–12.

[28] Clifford Putney, *Muscular Christianity: Manhood and Sports in Protestant America, 1880–1920* (Cambridge, MA: Harvard University Press, 2001), 41.

[29] Nathan D. Showalter, "The End of a Crusade: The Student Volunteer Movement for Foreign Missions and the Great War" (ThD diss., Harvard University, 1990), abstract [no page number], 12–13, 261.

[30] Steuer, "Pursuit of an 'Unparalleled Opportunity,'" 454–55, 458, 473.

Suggested Further Reading

Abel, Jonathan H. *Faith in the Fight: Religion and the American Soldier in the Great War.* Princeton, NJ: Princeton University Press, 2010.

Anderson, Paul B. *No East or West.* Edited by Donald E. Davis. Paris: YMCA Press, 1985.

Barnes, M. Craig. "John R. Mott: A Conversionist in a Pluralist World." PhD diss., University of Chicago, 1992.

Copeland, Jeffrey C., and Yan Xu, editors. *The YMCA at War: Collaboration and Conflict during the World Wars.* Lanham, MD: Lexington Books, 2018.

Cunningham, James W. *The Gates of Hell: The Great Sobor of the Russian Orthodox Church, 1917–1918.* Edited by Keith and Grace Dyrud. Minneapolis: Minnesota Mediterranean and East European Monographs, 2002.

Davis, Donald E., and Eugene P. Trani. "The American YMCA and the Russian Revolution." *Slavic Review* 33, no. 4 (September 1974): 469–91.

———. *The First Cold War: The Legacy of Woodrow Wilson in U.S.-Soviet Relations.* Columbia: University of Missouri Press, 2002.

Destivelle, Hyacinthe. *The Moscow Council (1917–1918): The Creation of the Conciliar Institutions of the Russian Orthodox Church.* Notre Dame, IN: University of Notre Dame Press, 2015.

Foglesong, David S. *The American Mission and the "Evil Empire": The Crusade for a "Free Russia" since 1881.* New York: Cambridge University Press, 2007.

Hopkins, C. Howard. *History of the YMCA in North America.* New York: Association Press, 1951.

———. *John R. Mott, 1865–1955: A Biography.* Grand Rapids, MI: Eerdmans, 1979.

Latourette, Kenneth Scott. *World Service: A History of the Foreign Work and World Service of the Young Men's Christian Associations of the United States and Canada.* New York: Association Press, 1957.

Long, John W., and C. Howard Hopkins. "The Church and the Russian Revolution: Conversations of John R. Mott with Orthodox Church Leaders, June–July 1917." *St. Vladimir's Theological Quarterly* 20, no. 3 (1976): 161–80.

Miller, Matthew Lee. *The American YMCA and Russian Culture: The Preservation and Expansion of Orthodox Christianity, 1900–1940.* Lanham, MD: Lexington Books, 2013.

———. "The American YMCA and Russian Politics: Critics and Supporters of Socialism, 1900–1940." In *New Perspectives on Russian-American Relations*, edited by William Benton Whisenhunt and Norman E. Saul, 161–77. New York: Routledge, 2015.

Mott, John R. *Addresses and Papers of John R. Mott.* 6 vols. New York: Association Press, 1946.

Parker, Michael. *The Kingdom of Character: The Student Volunteer Movement for Foreign Missions (1886–1926).* Lanham, MD: University Press of America, 1998.

Pierard, Richard V. "John R. Mott and the Rift in the Ecumenical Movement During World War I." *Journal of Ecumenical Studies* 23, no. 4 (Fall 1986): 601–20.

Polk, Jennifer A. "Constructive Efforts: The American Red Cross and YMCA in Revolutionary and Civil War Russia, 1917–1924." PhD diss., University of Toronto, 2012.

Ramsey, Dwayne George. "College Evangelists and Foreign Missions: The Student Volunteer Movement, 1886–1920." PhD diss., University of California–Davis, 1988.

Saul, Norman E. *Concord and Conflict: The United States and Russia, 1867–1914.* Lawrence: University Press of Kansas, 1996.

———. *The Life and Times of Charles R. Crane, 1858–1939: American Businessman, Philanthropist, and a Founder of Russian Studies in America.* Lanham, MD: Lexington Books, 2012.

———. *War and Revolution: The United States and Russia, 1914–1921.* Lawrence: University Press of Kansas, 2001.

Showalter, Nathan D. *The End of a Crusade: The Student Volunteer Movement for Foreign Missions and the Great War.* Lanham, MD: Scarecrow Press, 1998.

Steuer, Kenneth Andrew. *Pursuit of an "Unparalleled Opportunity": The American YMCA and Prisoner-of-War Diplomacy among the Central Power Nations during World War I, 1914–1923.* New York: Columbia University Press, 2009.

Taft, William Howard, et al., eds. *Service with Fighting Men: An Account of the Work of the American Young Men's Christian Associations in the World War.* 2 vols. New York: Association Press, 1922–24.

Tyrrell, Ian. *Reforming the World: The Creation of America's Moral Empire.* Princeton, NJ: Princeton University Press, 2010.

EDITOR'S NOTE

In his documents, John R. Mott refers to dates using the Gregorian calendar, rather than the Julian calendar, which was in use in Russia at the time of the Root Mission. The editor's introduction and footnotes also refer to dates according to the Gregorian calendar in use today. The editor has preserved the grammar and style of the original documents; however, a number of spellings have been converted to contemporary forms in order to promote readability.

ACKNOWLEDGMENTS

Please allow me to express my gratitude to a number of people who have supported the development of this book. My wife, Terri, and our daughters, Claire and Amelia, encourage me every day. Theofanis Stavrou, Mark Elliott, and Mark Noll continue to provide assistance and inspiration: my appreciation for each of them grows as the number of years since graduate school increases. Thank you to Norman Saul and Ben Whisenhunt for creating and editing the book series *Americans in Revolutionary Russia*, and to the staff of Slavica Publishers. I deeply appreciate my colleagues at Northwestern, especially fellow historians Jonathan Den Hartog and Jonathan Loopstra, and our administrators. The Association for the Study of Eastern Christian History and Culture and the Association for Slavic, East European, and Eurasian Studies each provide a collegial atmosphere for the active exchange of ideas. Historians are lost without librarians and archivists: my thanks go to Ryan Bean of the Kautz Family YMCA Archives and the stellar library staff at the University of Northwestern–St. Paul. Pavel Tribunsky and Joan Duffy of Yale Divinity Library provided assistance in locating photographs. Finally, thank you to Jackie Lofstad and Abby Erickson, outstanding teaching assistants, for technical assistance.

RECENT EXPERIENCES AND IMPRESSIONS IN RUSSIA

EXTRACTS FROM CORRESPONDENCE AND ADDRESSES OF JOHN R. MOTT, MEMBER OF THE SPECIAL DIPLOMATIC MISSION OF THE UNITED STATES TO RUSSIA, MAY–AUGUST, 1917

BY
JOHN R. MOTT

124 EAST TWENTY-EIGHTH STREET
NEW YORK

LETTER FROM JOHN R. MOTT REGARDING A MOST URGENT NEED IN RUSSIA

U. S. S. *BUFFALO*

Near Unimak Pass, Aleutian Islands,
July 30, 1917

Russia has called to the colors since the war began not less than 13,200,000 men. This constitutes the largest army assembled by any one nation in the history of the world. Of this vast number it is estimated that fully 2,000,000 have already been killed or have died as the result of wounds or diseases occasioned by the war. Another 2,000,000 are today prisoners of war in Germany, Austria-Hungary, Bulgaria, and Turkey. Another 2,000,000 may be classified as permanently ineffective, chiefly those who have been seriously mutilated in warfare or shattered by disease. This leaves 7,200,000 men as comprising the total strength of the Russian army of today. Some authorities whom I consulted give a somewhat lower figure, but more would place it even higher. Of this army of today, probably 2,100,000 are to be found in the seventy corps on the European front and the five on the Asiatic front; 1,000,000 in the depots or reserves; 1,000,000 in connection with garrisons and communications—thus leaving a little over 3,000,000 in training, on leave or otherwise not immediately available for military operations, but potentially a most important asset. On this vast host of Russian men and boys rests the tremendous responsibility of maintaining and pressing the war on the long drawn out eastern front. The effectiveness and faithfulness with which they perform this critical duty will determine, far more largely than we in America have realized, the extent of the exertions and sacrifices, and the laying down of life and substance, of the American people in connection with the great struggle. Whatever can be done, therefore, to ensure and develop the highest working efficiency and truly triumphant spirit of the Russian soldiers has a most direct, practical, and vital bearing on the destiny of America and the other Allies. As a member of the

Special Diplomatic Mission to Russia which had been charged by President Wilson[1] with the responsibility of studying ways in which America and Russia might best cooperate in the war, I gave not a little attention, in accordance with the wish of our Chairman, Mr. Root,[2] to the consideration of this large and pressing problem.

That there is imperative need of instituting measures for rendering practical service to the millions of Russian men and boys under arms or in uniform there can be no question in the mind of anyone who has first-hand knowledge of conditions. This need existed before the Russian Revolution.[3] A similar need had been recognized in all the other Allied armies, and with greater or less thoroughness was being met; but, notwithstanding the most helpful activities of such agencies as the zemstvos unions,[4] there has been lacking in the Russian army from the beginning an agency to specialize on the physical, mental, social, and moral betterment of the men as has been done in so many of the other countries by the Young Men's Christian Association. The Russian Revolution has greatly accentuated the need. From the nature of the case the minds of multitudes of Russian soldiers have been more or less absorbed with the political and the social issues thrust upon them by the Revolution. Moreover, the subtle, able forces of German intrigue have taken advantage of these unsettled conditions and have waged a really masterly propaganda among large numbers of the troops in the garrisons, in the training camps, and, to a larger degree than might be thought possible, at the front. As one studies these troops wherever they are congregated throughout Russia or Siberia, at the front or at the base, one is impressed by the vast numbers who either are not occupied at all with activities related to the war or are devoting themselves to aimless and unprofitable political discussion. The practical problem, stated in a sentence, is: Shall these millions of young men and boys in garrisons, in reserve camps and at the fighting front spend the five or more leisure hours which they have each day in idleness, in dissipation, and in unprofitable or weakening agitation, or shall they devote these spare hours to healthful physical and social recreation, growth in knowledge and working efficiency, and unselfish service to their fellowmen? This war has shown the supreme importance of morale. Napoleon went so far as to maintain that morale counts for an army as three to one. How important is it that everything possible be done during these coming months

---

[1] Woodrow Wilson (1856–1924) served as President of the United States from 1913–21.

[2] Elihu Root (1845–1937) led the diplomatic mission to Russia in 1917. Earlier he had served as secretary of state (1905–09) and as United States senator from New York (1909–15).

[3] Mott is referring to the "February Revolution," which led to the abdication of Emperor Nicholas II on March 15, 1917.

[4] During the war, zemstvo unions served as catalysts for local self-governing organizations and individuals to offer medical services and other supplies for soldiers, and aid for refugees and orphans.

to improve the morale, to strengthen the discipline, and to raise the spirit of our comrades in Russia.

The marvelous success achieved by the Young Men's Christian Association in the British, Canadian, and Australasian armies not only on the west front, but also in Egypt, Mesopotamia, Saloniki, and on the Gallipoli Peninsula, in the wonderful French army, as well as in the newly-forming American army, has demonstrated the adaptability of this organization for meeting the situation in Russia. I am glad to state that even before I arrived in Russia on this last visit some of our American Association secretaries, who have long been at work there in the prisoner-of-war camps, had become so impressed by the need and by the urgency of the situation that they, without knowledge of each other's action, had already inaugurated work among the Russian soldiers at a number of points as widely separated as Petrograd[5] on the west, Tomsk and Irkutsk in Siberia, and Tashkent in Turkestan.[6] These efforts met with the instant and enthusiastic approval of both soldiers and officers. To promote recreation and the physical conditioning of the men, football, volley ball, track athletics, relay races, and aquatics had been introduced. The educational work included language schools, courses for other useful studies, libraries, reading rooms, lectures, and moving picture shows. Wise use was being made of high-grade theatrical plays. The musical features of the work were also most welcome. The moral and religious life of the soldiers received sympathetic and careful attention. Wherever possible, the men were being enlisted in unselfish service among their fellows. As I studied these experiments I asked myself, Why is not this work reproducible throughout the entire Russian army?

In order to ascertain whether the Russians would welcome American cooperation through such an agency as the Association, I had interviews with a number of persons. I discussed the matter at length with Prince Lvov,[7] the Premier, and found him most intelligently sympathetic. Mr. Tereshchenko,[8] Minister of Foreign Affairs, responded heartily to the suggestion. I had but a few moments with the minister of War and Marine, Mr. Kerensky,[9] and arranged to go into the subject more fully with him at his leisure, but he had not yet returned from the front when I was obliged to start

---

[5] The Russian city of St. Petersburg was known as Petrograd from 1914–24 (and as Leningrad from 1924–91).

[6] Turkestan was a region of the Russian Empire in central Asia.

[7] Georgy E. Lvov (1861–1925) was the prime minister of Russia from March 15 to July 20, 1917. The prime minister led the Provisional Government, the temporary government of Russia, from March 15 to November 8, 1917.

[8] Mikhail I. Tereshchenko (1886–1956) served in the Provisional Government as minister of finance (March–May) and minister of foreign affairs (May–November).

[9] Alexander F. Kerensky (1881–1970) served in the Provisional Government as minister of justice (March 16–May 1), minister of war and navy (May 18–September 14), and prime minister (July 20–November 8).

back to America. Other members of the War Ministry, however, have indicated to us their hearty approval. The Chief of the General Staff assured me that he and his colleagues would welcome the help of this American Association. With the assistance of Mr. Harte, our chief Association representative in Eastern Europe, many of the Soldiers' Deputies, as well as other soldiers, were interviewed and brought together in groups for consultation. They entered into the new plans with the keenest interest and assured us of their earnest cooperation. In view of such a uniformly favorable response preliminary steps were taken before I left Russia to constitute a National Committee to have general supervision of the extension of the Association Movement throughout the Russian army. Prince Kropotkin[10] will probably serve as chairman. Other men of large influence who command the full confidence of soldiers and officers will be members. As the demand for this work was so very urgent, I diverted from the prisoner-of-war work in Russia and Siberia ten of our best American secretaries, and arranged for them to devote themselves to the work for the Russian soldiers. A cablegram was sent to America asking that certain other workers who had been in Russia and who were more or less acquainted with the Russian language and Russian conditions be dispatched to Russia as soon as possible to help meet this unique opportunity. One of our most efficient secretaries in Siberia is bringing out a valuable booklet on Association principles and methods for army work and it is now being printed in Russian. Other pamphlets are also being planned, including a manual for the guidance of those who are to engage in this particular form of service.

All my investigations convinced me that the soldiers of Russia present to Americans possibly the largest single opportunity among the countless doors for constructive service which have been open to us during the war. Here is a field that stretches one-third of the way around the world. It involves literally millions of men and boys—as many as the Association is today serving in the combined armies of Britain, Canada, America, and France. It is wide open to our friendly approach. It is a most responsive field. At many points the Russian army reminded me quite as much of older boys as of mature men, and these hosts of boys, and the men too for that matter, can be led anywhere by workers of warm hearts, wise heads, and an unselfish spirit. They are most responsive to kindness. Very many of them are eager for self-development, are truly idealistic, and possess a genuinely religious nature. It is not an optional matter whether we of America shall enter this wide and effectual door; it is obligatory that we do so. By this I mean that it is a clear duty because a need known and ability to meet that need constitute a clear call of duty. To deal in any worthy or adequate way with this boundless opportunity means that we must send over to Russia as soon as possible hundreds of the best qualified workers whom we can find. The difficulties and temptations which await these workers are so subtle and serious that we should send only men of established character, of rich experience, and

---

[10] Peter A. Kropotkin (1842–1921) was an aristocrat, intellectual, and political activist.

of undiscourageable enthusiasm. It may be found wise and practicable to establish a language school where all of these workers can spend at least a short period on arriving in Russia, although a man should begin his study of the Russian language the day he decides to enter this field. For every American secretary there should be at least ten Russian workers.

It would be difficult to over-state the urgency of this extraordinary situation. The late autumn and the winter months will constitute the most critical testing period. If these men can be afforded pleasant and profitable occupation during this trying time it will ensure conservation of probably the greatest single asset of the Allied cause; whereas, if through the influence of counter-revolutionary forces, of German intrigue, and of disintegrating habits of dissipation and idleness, the great Russian army should be permitted to dissolve or be riven with seams of weakness, the most disastrous consequences will follow. Just now America, as no other nation, holds the key to the situation. Her prompt recognition of the Revolutionary Government and her genuine and expressed desire to do anything in her power to help Russia, make the Russian people peculiarly hospitable to American ideas and workers. It is well for us to keep reminding ourselves that the Russians have long been fighting our battles for us, and this at a terrific cost. Anything which we find it possible to do in the way of giving money and men to extend a great, practical, unselfish ministry of this kind, we should promptly do. Such a service on our part during the critical months which lie directly before us, together with the unobtrusive, truly Christ-like work which our secretaries have accomplished during the last two years among the millions of Russian prisoners in the Middle Countries, will accomplish more than all other influences combined to open the door for the sending forth of similar influences during the years following the war—years in which the plastic New Russia may be so profoundly and so permanently influenced.

SPEECH BY JOHN R. MOTT AT A DINNER GIVEN BY MR. EMANUEL NOBEL AT HIS HOME IN PETROGRAD, JUNE 21, 1917

Mr. Nobel,[11] and Gentlemen: After the felicitous words of our honored and beloved Ambassador, Mr. Francis,[12] it is not necessary that I should reiterate the expression of deepest gratitude of my associates and myself for the gracious and generous hospitality of our host. We esteem it a great honor and privilege to meet in the home of one who is associated in our thoughts with so many valuable and constructive services for mankind, and also to have fellowship this evening with this particular group of men of wide outlook and of responsiveness to the highest purposes which move men. It is an added source of satisfaction to those of us who belong to the Special Mission, sent by President Wilson to Russia, to find here tonight the members of the Council of the *Miyak* Society.[13] One of the purposes of our Mission, as emphasized by President Wilson, is that we shall study ways in which Russia and America can best cooperate. The *Miyak* and its work constitute one of the finest illustrations of unselfish cooperation between large-minded and large-hearted citizens of these two great nations. It has been an inspiring sight through all the recent years to observe how in this organization the streams of benevolence, of experience, of idealism, and of practical working efficiency of the two nationalities have blended to the mutual helpfulness of both peoples. Thus while we of the Special Mission from America are studying and discussing the subject of cooperation between the two peoples, you of

---

[11] Emanuel L. Nobel (1859–1932) was a wealthy Swedish-Russian oil industrialist and philanthropist.

[12] David R. Francis (1850–1927) served as US ambassador to Russia from 1916 to 1917. For the account of his experiences as ambassador, see his book *Russia from the American Embassy*, ed. Vladimir V. Noskov (Bloomington, IN: Slavica, 2019).

[13] The *Mayak* (or *Miyak*, Lighthouse) in St. Petersburg (1900–18), formally known as the Society for the Promotion of Moral, Intellectual, and Physical Development of Young Men, was the most visible expression of the YMCA's work in Russia. New York businessman James Stokes (1841–1918) provided the vision and funding, while Franklin Augustus Gaylord (1856–1943) served as program director. The *Mayak* provided athletic, educational, cultural, and religious programs for hundreds of young men.

this beneficent society, both the members of your Council and your able secretaries as well as your unfailing supporters here and in America, are actually exemplifying a splendid cooperation.

Although this is my fourth visit to Russia, it is the first time that I have had the opportunity to travel throughout the vast breadth of the country as it stretches from ocean to ocean. As I have journeyed from Vladivostok to Petrograd and as I have considered more thoroughly than ever before the needs and possibilities of the great cities of Russia, I have been asking myself day by day: Why should there not be a chain of *Miyak*s bringing the helpful ministries of this Society to the young men and boys of all the principal Russian cities? My study of the valuable and constructive work accomplished by the *Miyak* in Petrograd has convinced me that what you have been doing here is reproducible, and the question may well be raised whether the time is not at hand when this helpful agency should be transplanted gradually, yet as rapidly as practicable, first to Moscow and then to other leading centers of population.

We are living in the most eventful and critical moment in the life of Russia. It is a time of upheaval and readjustment to be followed in the near future by a period of significant reconstruction. At such a moment it is fitting that we re-examine the foundations of greatness in the life of a nation. What is it that makes a nation truly great? Not the extent of its territory or dominions; not the size of its population; not the number of its millionaires; not the strength and output of its industrial establishment—none of these constitutes the real source of greatness in a nation. Moreover, education by itself, in the common acceptation of the term, cannot ensure true national greatness. We all know that one of the best educated nations in the world, if not the best, is possibly the most dangerous nation. Education simply sharpens the weapons and makes one more skillful in their use—but uses them for what and against what? It was said of the brilliant Lorenzo de' Medici[14] that "he was cultured yet corrupt, wise yet cruel, spending the morning writing a sonnet in praise of virtue and spending the night in vice." I care not how well educated a man may be, if he has low ideals, a corrupt heart and an ungoverned will, he is a menace to society and a seam of weakness in the life of the nation. What then makes a nation truly great? The ideals, the character, and the spirit of a people; and history shows that ideas cannot be placed and held at their highest, that character cannot be made symmetrical and strong, and that the spirit cannot be made free and triumphant apart from the help of true religion. Therefore, the work of a society like the *Miyak*, which corresponds to the Young Men's Christian Association of America and other lands, is striking at the heart of the most critical problems in the life of the nation. What could be more important than to make sure that such agencies are securely planted, ably led and generously supported in all of the principal cities of Russia?

---

[14] Lorenzo de' Medici (1449–92) was a political and financial leader in Florence during the Renaissance era.

There is another field in Russia for the work of the Young Men's Christian Association which presents an even more urgent appeal at this present hour and that is the millions of Russian young men in the army and navy. The war has reached its most critical stage. The young men in the training camps, in the reserve camps, and in the trenches, and likewise on the war vessels and at the naval stations, will determine more than any other one factor the outcome. How desirable it is that everything possible be done to preserve among them a high morale, efficient action, and a conquering spirit. The experience in the other great armies of the Allies has shown conclusively that the work of these Associations has accomplished wonders in ensuring these highly desirable and essential results. Such work has spread in the British army until now it is conducted at two thousand different points. Since the war began they have expended in support of such Associations nearly four million pounds. Thousands of efficient secretaries and tens of thousands of unselfish volunteer workers are busily engaged in bringing this helpful ministry to their five millions of soldiers. It has been introduced with like success into the brilliant French army, that army which has made such a remarkable record in this war. At hundreds of points in the garrison cities, in the reserve camps, and now quite near the fighting lines, they have established these Associations, known as *Foyers du Soldat*.[15] Since coming to Petrograd I have received a cable gram from France asking us to secure and send to them five hundred Americans, to enable them to extend this society more widely and rapidly throughout the entire French army. Recently also the Italian Government has permitted the Association to begin similar work among their soldiers. A remarkable service has been accomplished by this society in that army which has had to endure so much suffering and strain, the one in Mesopotamia. The day that America decided to enter the war a telegram was sent to President Wilson placing at the disposal of the American Government the organization of the Young Men's Christian Association. He accepted the offer with most hearty appreciation and has done everything in his power to facilitate the work. He has issued a special Executive Order calling upon the officers in the American army to give the Association every practical facility for its work. During the past few weeks the Association has called upon and received from the American people, rich and poor, for the support of this work in the American army for the first year over four million dollars.

We have been glad to learn that at several points in different parts of Russia within the last few weeks similar work has been organized for the Russian soldiers. Is this not a most opportune time to spread these agencies for the physical, mental, and moral betterment of the soldiers among all parts of the great Russian army and into the navy as well? I do not fear for the soldiers when they are fighting or when they are drilling. The time concerning which I have anxiety is their leisure hours. Every soldier has a number of spare hours each day. Shall these hours be spent in idleness, in

---

[15] Soldiers' Homes.

dissipation, and in unprofitable agitation; or shall they be spent in helpful recreation, in growth in knowledge and mental efficiency, in strengthening of character, and in unselfish service among one's fellows? The Young Men's Christian Association has shown itself able to answer this vital question in the right way. Therefore, it has the unqualified endorsement of the generals and admirals of the armies and navies of the various Allied countries where it has been introduced. We bespeak for this organization the hearty approval and cooperation of the discerning leaders of Russia and, in particular, of the officers, soldiers, and sailors. Let me in closing express on behalf of the American people our desire to cooperate with our friends in Russia in every way in our power to facilitate the development of this helpful movement among your soldiers and sailors and likewise among other classes of your young men. We in America feel that during the last three years you have indeed been fighting our battles for us. You have paid tremendous prices which we can never adequately repay. Anything, therefore, which we can possibly do to strengthen your hands at this momentous hour, when with us and the other Allies you press on to achieve the full purpose of the war, we will gladly do.

LETTER FROM MAJOR-GENERAL H. L. SCOTT[16] TO JOHN R. MOTT

Washington, D.C., August 10, 1917.

Dear Dr. Mott:

I hope you will push the plan of spreading the work of the Young Men's Christian Association throughout the Russian Army. Get the facts before the President. This is a matter in which our Government should cooperate at once. It will also appeal strongly to men and women of means in America.

For years I have been intimately acquainted with the good, practical work done by the Young Men's Christian Association in the American Army and Navy. I have seen its helpful activities in the Philippines, in Cuba, on our Mexican Border, and elsewhere. We could not have done without it. It has been managed in such a broadminded and wise way that it has been well received by officers and enlisted men whose views on other questions have differed materially. I have just seen much of the Russian Army on the German, Austrian, and Romanian fronts, and also in many garrison towns of Russia and Siberia, and am convinced that the Association work should be immediately organized in this great army in order to ensure the contentment and efficiency of the men, to raise their morale, and to help counteract the intriguing propaganda which is doing so much to unsettle them.

The Romanian situation must not be forgotten. It is of tremendous importance. I hear good reports about your work in the French Army. I am not surprised that General Pershing[17] wishes to have it rapidly extended.

---

[16] Hugh L. Scott (1853–1934) served as a career military officer for the US Army in a variety of settings, including the western United States, Cuba, and the Philippines. Scott was chief of staff for the US Army from 1914–17 and was a member of the Root Mission with John R. Mott.

[17] John J. Pershing (1860–1948) commanded the American Expeditionary Force in Europe from 1917–18.

I need not emphasize the importance of your choosing the best qualified men to take charge of this work in the armies of our Allies. They could render no greater service to our country and our cause, even from a military point of view, than to help build up and save the power of these millions of men on whom the great strain comes. Such a work requires the best men you can find.

Sincerely yours,
H. L. Scott,
Chief of Staff of the United States Army.
Dr. John R. Mott,
124 East 28th Street,
New York City.

LETTER FROM JOHN R. MOTT REGARDING RECENT RELIGIOUS DEVELOPMENTS IN RUSSIA

U.S.S. *Buffalo*,
Okhotsk Sea, July 24, 1917.

As you know, President Wilson early in May appointed a Special Diplomatic Mission to Russia consisting of nine men: Elihu Root, as Chairman, Major General Hugh L. Scott, Rear Admiral James H. Glennon,[18] Charles R. Crane,[19] Cyrus H. McCormick,[20] Samuel R. Bertron,[21] James Duncan,[22] Charles Edward Russell,[23] and myself. In his instructions the President charged us with two principal duties—to convey to the Government and people of Russia the expression of the sympathy and good will of the American Government and people; and to consider ways in which the two governments can best cooperate in the work of achieving the objects of war. We left Washington on May 15 and reached Petrograd on June 13. After spending four weeks in most intense and profitable work, we have accomplished the main purpose of our Mission, and are now on our way home. Not until we have rendered our official report to the President can we speak of the political and diplomatic aspects of our work. There are, however, certain impressions and experiences on which we are free

---

[18] James H. Glennon (1857–1940) served as a career officer in the US Navy and reached the rank of rear admiral.

[19] Charles R. Crane (1858–1939), heir to an industrial fortune, promoted a range of political, cultural, and philanthropic ventures, especially those connected to Slavic and Arab cultures.

[20] Cyrus H. McCormick, Jr. (1859–1936), led the McCormick Harvesting Machine Company and the International Harvester Company as president.

[21] Samuel R. Bertron (1865–1938) was a lawyer and investment banker.

[22] James Duncan (1857–1928), granite cutter and union leader, was vice president of the American Federation of Labor.

[23] Charles Edward Russell (1860–1941), journalist and writer, participated in the Socialist Party of America, but was expelled from the party due to his support of US intervention in the World War.

to comment. It has occurred to me that you might be interested in my observations and contacts in connection with the Church while in Russia.

The attention of the world has been so much absorbed with the political and social revolution in Russia that comparatively little has been said regarding what is in some respects equally remarkable—the wonderful religious changes now in progress in that country, especially in relation to the Russian Orthodox Church. The High Procurator of the Holy Synod[24] told me just before I left Russia that greater and more significant changes had been effected in the Church during the preceding month than in the past two hundred years. He insisted, and the facts would seem to support him, that these changes have amounted to nothing less than a revolution. In the first place, religious tolerance has at last been achieved in Russia. All religions now stand on an equality. Men everywhere are free to worship God according to their own convictions and forms. They are also at liberty to organize their own religious associations, and to conduct their work without restriction. Even the Jews now have equal rights before the law and an end has come to the long tragedy of persecutions, humiliations, and massacres. The attitude of any Christian nation toward the Jews is among the most searching tests of the character of its freedom. Many other sects for generations most severely oppressed have come out into the larger life and liberty.

The Russian Orthodox Church is undergoing a complete reorganization. The process may best be defined as a democratization of the Church. There has come a complete break with the old bureaucratic regime. The power of the Church is being decentralized. Its provincial government will be rapidly developed. Parish, district, and diocesan councils and committees are being formed or reconstituted, and have been given the freedom and authority necessary to ensure the best life of the Church. The democratic principle has been applied to the election of many of the clergy. Already twelve bishops have been elected by popular vote, including those of Petrograd and Moscow. A plan is being perfected by which the Holy Synod will be elected by the Church itself, through a properly constituted national assembly.

The various extraordinary changes which are taking place so rapidly in the outer organization and administration of the Church are but a reflection of an equally striking internal reformation. The Russian Church undoubtedly sank to its lowest level of life and influence during the last year, in connection with the shocking and almost unbelievable Rasputin[25] scandal. With the shaking off of the old servitude, which has come with the great Revolution, the Russian Church has broken out into new life. Questionable practices have been abandoned, old corruptions have been

---

[24] The ober-procurator was the imperial government official who presided over the Holy Synod, the leadership body of the Russian Orthodox Church. Here Mott is referring to Vladimir Lvov, who served in this role from March 3 to July 24, 1917.

[25] Grigory Rasputin (1869–1916), known as a faith healer, was invited by Emperor Nicholas II to help his son, Alexei, who suffered from hemophilia. Rasputin was killed in 1916 after many expressed concern over his lifestyle and his influence on the imperial family.

cast aside, and the work of purification is advancing apace. A special commission is at work on purifying the life of the seminaries. In many quarters one finds refreshing signs of spiritual quickening.

One of the most hopeful developments is that in the direction of increasing the working efficiency of the Church. The Great Sobor, or Council, held in Moscow in the month of June,[26] devoted itself throughout the entire ten days to this task. It accomplished a solid constructive work in the direction of improving the parish life of the churches, in defining new relations which should exist between the Church and the State, in determining wise plans for the development of parish schools, in calling out more largely the latent lay forces, and above all, in devising ways and means of improving the work of the clergy.

A strong and representative commission is at work revising the curriculum of the ecclesiastical academies and seminaries. Measures are being taken also to transform certain of the monasteries, which had passed into a stage of decline and lifelessness, into institutions for scholastic research, and for the uplifting of the life of the Church through carrying to the people the Gospel by word and print. That all these progressive movements and tendencies may be strengthened and carried forward to full fruition, it has been decided that there shall be held, beginning late in August, in the city of Moscow, an Extraordinary Council of the Russian Church. A Preparation Committee, composed of the Holy Synod and some forty of the other most influential leaders of the Church, is at work perfecting the plans for this gathering, and will continue its labors until the Council assembles.

Another sign of large encouragement is the movement in the direction of closer Christian fellowship and unity among the different Christian bodies in Russia. It has been decided to invite to the great Council, so soon to assemble, representatives of the Old Believers,[27] the principal dissenting sect in Russia—a sect numbering over twelve millions of members which has been bitterly persecuted for over two hundred years—and the invitation has been accepted. Negotiations of peculiar interest and significance have been entered into between the ecclesiastics of the Orthodox and Roman Catholic Communions. As a result, it is probable that the latter body will hold a Church Council or Assembly at the time that the great Council of the Orthodox Church is in session. Attention should also be called to the multiplying sympathetic points of contact between Protestant Christians and the Russian Church. An

---

[26] This statement by Mott is not precise: he did not attend the council, which opened after the completion of the Root Mission on August 28, 1917, and ended September 20, 1918, but the event he did experience was the All-Russian Congress of Clergy and Laity, June 16–25, 1917, which made preparations for the council. This imprecision may have been due to an error in translation: the Russian word *sobor* can be translated as council or cathedral, depending on the context.

[27] The Old Believers separated from the leadership of the patriarch of the Russian Orthodox Church during and after the time of Patriarch Nikon's reforms in the seventeenth century.

illustration is that of my own experience while in Russia. I will enlarge upon this because it will serve to enforce what has been said regarding the striking change which has come over the religious situation in Russia.

Within a few days after we reached Russia, I was invited, along with my associate, Mr. Crane, to attend the Great Sobor of the Russian Orthodox Church then in session in Moscow. By Sobor is meant what would be called in the Presbyterian Church at home a General Assembly, or in the Episcopal Church a General Convention, or in the Methodist Church a General Conference. These are poor analogies, because this Sobor is one of unique importance, being the first representative national gathering held by the Russian Church in a period of over two hundred years—that is, since 1682. It was attended by 1072 official delegates, each one hundred parishes being entitled to send as representatives two priests and two laymen. In addition to the delegates sent by the parishes, the Holy Synod had appointed as delegates several leading bishops. Every part of Russia was represented. During the ten days that the Sobor was in session part of the time was devoted to sectional meetings and the rest to plenary meetings. The recommendations of the section gatherings were presented to the main sessions, where they were discussed and adopted. Archbishop Platon,[28] formerly at the head of the Russian Church in America, invited me to give a formal address before the Sobor. As good fortune would have it, I found among the delegates Father Alexandrov,[29] the Russian priest at San Francisco, who speaks English very well. We had met before, having attended together one of our Association conventions in America. He proved an ideal interpreter. I spoke for an hour, bringing first a message of gratitude from America to the Russian Christians; secondly, a message of solicitude and caution to the Russian Church in this critical hour in the life of the nation; and thirdly, a message of hope or reassurance. My address was received throughout with most evident sympathy and enthusiasm. At least a score of times during the address the entire audience arose, this being a sign of most signal approval. It was a striking fact that these manifestations came in connection with the most significant and vital points. At the end of the address the delegates rose instantly and joined in one of their church hymns, calling upon the Holy Spirit to come upon us. They followed this with the famous Russian song, "Many Years," and this was succeeded by another spiritual hymn. Then came four speeches in response to the message and in appreciation of the fact that Mr. Crane and I had come to them as the representatives of President Wilson and of the American people. The first of these speeches was made by the president of the Sobor, a distinguished professor of Moscow University. The next speech was

---

[28] Archbishop Platon (Rozhdestvensky, 1866–1934) led the Russian Orthodox churches in the United States from 1907–14 and later from 1922–34. At the time of the Root Mission, he was in Russia serving as a member of the Holy Synod.

[29] Vladimir V. Alexandrov (1871–1945) served as an Orthodox priest in San Francisco and other locations in the United States.

by Bishop Andrew of Ufa,[30] speaking on behalf of the Bishops. He was followed by Prince Trubetskoy,[31] who is likewise a professor in the University. The last address of thanks was made by the High Procurator of the Holy Synod. In no gathering of Protestant Christians, or those of any other communion, have I ever been received more whole-heartedly.

A few days later, on my return to Petrograd, another opportunity presented itself—one which seems almost incredible. I was invited by the High Procurator to give an address before the Holy Synod and other leaders of the Russian Church, who had assembled to lay plans for the Extraordinary Council of the Church to be held at the end of August. I began by congratulating the leaders of the Russian Church on its achievements throughout the centuries, giving in outline the principal results accomplished. Then I congratulated them on the present opportunities before the Church in Russia and beyond its borders, and likewise upon the grave difficulties which beset the Church in this time of upheaval and change, reminding them of the value of difficulties in calling out our latent energies and in deepening our acquaintance with God. After that I congratulated them on the future, showing them why the best days of the Russian Church lie in the years just before us. The next heading of my address dealt with the eight most distinctive contributions which American Christianity has made to the common Christianity of the world. One had in view in such a presentation the bringing of influence to bear indirectly on the Russian Church itself, because the strong points in the religious life of America are among the very aspects of the Russian Church which most need to receive constructive attention. These outstanding leaders of the Christian forces of the country listened with unmistakable sympathy, and when I had finished, the President, Archbishop Platon, also the High Procurator and others expressed their sincere appreciation. I was assured by those present that, so far as the Church is concerned, the way is now open in Russia for our Association Movement. While I was present with the Holy Synod two significant steps were taken. It was voted to hold in Moscow, beginning about the end of August, the Extraordinary Council of the Russian Church, to which I have already referred. They also agreed unanimously that one of the objects of the Council is to facilitate the union of the Orthodox Church and the Old Believers. A delegate from the latter body who was present responded in the finest spirit to the overtures of the Orthodox Church. When one thinks of the terrible persecutions which the Old Believers have suffered at the hands of the State Church, the drawing together of these great communions seems indeed wonderful. It will interest you to know that the meeting on this day was held in

---

[30] Archbishop Andrew (Ukhtomsky) of Ufa (1872–1937) was a member of the Holy Synod during the Root Mission.

[31] Evgeny N. Trubetskoy (1863–1920) taught philosophy at the University of Moscow, and interacted with the ideas of his brother, Sergei N. Trubetskoy, and Vladimir Solovyov.

the home of Pobedonostsev,[32] the former, famous, most able, and much feared High Procurator of the Holy Synod. When I reflected on the reactionary, relentless, and cruel way in which he administered the affairs of the Church, I found it difficult to realize that I had actually been accorded such an opportunity, and that I had lived to see the day of so great a transformation.

With Mr. Crane I returned to Moscow to witness on July 4 a significant event—the election of the new Metropolitan.[33] We first saw the procession of ecclesiastics and delegates march to the Cathedral of Our Savior[34] where the election and the accompanying ceremonies were to take place. It was an impressive sight to witness this picturesque company bearing various sacred icons and other insignia of the Church, and also the surging crowds of peasants and towns-folk lining the streets and following the procession. Only the eight hundred delegates and the officiating church leaders were admitted to the floor of the Cathedral. Everybody else had to stand in the galleries and it was not easy to obtain tickets even for this privilege. On our arrival the day before, the members of the Sobor had voted unanimously to admit Mr. Crane and myself to the floor, because they regarded us as special ambassadors from the Christians of America. They, therefore, gave us a place of honor on the platform before the *ikonostas*.[35] The eight hundred delegates included men in every walk of life from princes to peasants. They constituted one of the most fascinating sights which I have witnessed in any gathering. First came the regular ritual service of the Russian Orthodox Church, closing with the Holy Communion. The Archbishop of Yaroslav officiated, and several bishops and other church dignitaries assisted. The service, which lasted nearly three hours, was conducted with great solemnity and reverence and with evident depth of feeling. In this respect I know of no body of Christians who surpass the Russians. On this day the singing was largely congregational. Over one-third of the time was spent in singing responses, chants, psalms, and hymns. It would be impossible to describe the effect of the united worship and praise of these hundreds of devout Christians. After the formal service was finished, the delegates proceeded at once to the election of the Metropolitan. This was conducted in the body of the church, and continued for several hours. It was a most orderly proceeding. There were four different ballot boxes to facilitate the casting of the votes. In the presence of the delegates and the crowds in the galleries the votes were counted. There were four or

---

[32] Konstantin Pobedonostsev (1827–1907), an influential conservative political leader, served as ober-procurator of the Holy Synod from 1880–1905.

[33] Metropolitan is a title given to the bishop of a leading city, such as Moscow.

[34] The Cathedral of Christ the Savior was the largest cathedral in Moscow, located along the Moscow River near the Kremlin. It was consecrated in 1883, destroyed in 1931, and rebuilt in the 1990s.

[35] *Ikonostas* is Russian for "icon screen," the wall of icons in rows which divides the sanctuary (space for the altar) from the nave (space for the congregation).

five candidates, the two highest in the list being Archbishop Tikhon,[36] who received 481 votes, and a prominent layman, Mr. Samarin,[37] who received 303. Archbishop Tikhon, the successful candidate, was for several years Bishop of the Russian Church in America, and before he left there became its first Archbishop. He is a man of the finest character, and his election met with general approval, although the principal rival candidate had a strong following. After the vote was announced by the officers of the election, the Bishops gave careful consideration to the result, and then came forward and endorsed the choice of the delegates. The whole company joined in the singing of the Te Deum. This was followed by the singing of "Many Years" for the newly elected Metropolitan.

Between the church service and the election Mr. Crane and I were summoned to go behind the altar, and while there Archpriest Lubimov[38] of Moscow presented each of us with a sacred icon, in view of the service which we had rendered Russia, and in recognition of our relation to the Christian Movement throughout the world. The icon presented to me is one representing our Lord and was taken from the *ikonostas* of the Uspensky Cathedral,[39] where it had been for centuries. It is one of the fourteenth century, and they told me it is priceless. You will recall this cathedral as one of the oldest in Russia, and the one in which the Czars were crowned. In presenting me the icon, the Archpriest quite clearly referred to the fact of my being a Protestant, but said that they recognized my oneness with them in our belief in the one Divine Savior. He also referred to the service which we have rendered during the war to the more than two million Russian prisoners in Germany and Austria-Hungary. He has a son, a graduate of Moscow University, who is in one of these prisoner-of-war camps in Germany. He told me that this son had written him repeatedly about the helpfulness of our Association, and that while in it he had learned the English language. I told him that we would arrange to have sent to his son from Copenhagen every two weeks a parcel of food. This moved the old man to tears.

Sunday, July 1, was also a notable day in the relations between the Russian Orthodox Church and American Protestant Christianity. Largely as a result of

---

[36] Archbishop Tikhon (Bellavin) served as a bishop in North America from 1898 to 1907 and was installed as Patriarch of Moscow and All Russia in November 1917. He died in 1925 and was canonized in 1989 by the Moscow Patriarchate.

[37] Alexander D. Samarin (1868–1932) was ober-procurator of the Holy Synod from July to September 1915.

[38] Archpriest (Protopresbyter) Nikolai A. Lubimov (1858–1924) served at the Uspensky (Assumption, Dormition) Cathedral in Moscow and as a member of the Holy Synod.

[39] The Uspensky (Assumption, Dormition) Cathedral is the largest cathedral inside the Moscow Kremlin; the most recent structure was consecrated in 1479. It has served as a central place of worship for the Russian Orthodox Church, and was the location for coronations of rulers and consecrations of bishops, metropolitans, and patriarchs.

the intercourse we had had with the leaders of the Russian Church in the Sobor at Moscow, and in the meeting with the Holy Synod, some of the Russian ecclesiastics expressed their desire to have a special service conducted in one of their principal churches in recognition of the presence and help of the American Mission. The Kazan Cathedral[40] on Nevsky Prospekt in Petrograd was selected as a most desirable place for the purpose. The service lasted from ten o'clock until about one. The saintly and noble Archbishop Platon, who did such a wonderful work for the cause of Christ in America, officiated at the service and celebrated Holy Communion. The majority of the members of our Mission attended, also members of the Railroad Commission of which Mr. Stevens[41] is Chairman, the American Ambassador and his staff, and several other Americans. We were given a prominent place to stand on the platform facing the choir. As the service advanced the attendance grew, until people were standing in all parts of the great enclosure and were massed in large numbers at the front. Many bishops, priests, archpriests, and deacons participated in the elaborate ritual, which I have never seen conducted more impressively than it was on this occasion. The choir sang not only the customary responses, but also a number of deeply moving selections. A most unusual circumstance was the fact that Archbishop Platon, while celebrating the Holy Communion did so in part in the English language. Moreover, about the middle of the service, Father Alexandrov, of San Francisco, who had been my interpreter at the important religious gatherings, read in English the gospel lesson for the day, and preached in English an effective sermon on the Good Samaritan. He called attention to the timeliness and great significance of the fact that America had come to them in this most critical moment in the history of Russia, and begged America indeed not to "pass by on the other side" Russia in her hour of need, but to be to her a good Samaritan. He said: "The Russian people know how to be grateful; they will never forget America's kindness."

As the service came towards its climax a most unusual thing took place. One of the priests came to the Americans and invited them to go behind the *ikonostas*, where we observed the Archbishop administer the Holy Communion in both kinds to bishops and priests who were present. Then some of our number were called forward and the Archbishop administered the Holy Communion to each of us. He also presented to each one of us a little loaf of the sacred, or blessed, bread. We then returned to the place where we had stood throughout the early part of the service. The closing moments were more overpowering than ever in impressiveness. Possibly the most moving part was when the vast audience broke out and sang together in

---

[40] The Kazan Cathedral stands near the center of the city. It was completed in 1811 and later served as a site to commemorate the 1812 Russian military victory over Napoleon Bonaparte's armies.

[41] John Frank Stevens (1853–1943), a prominent railroad engineer in the US, served as a consultant in Russia and other countries.

perfect unison and with deep feeling the Lord's Prayer. There followed a period of intercession, led by one of the priests, when they prayed for the army, for the President and people of the United States, for the Allies, for all the Americans present, for the Russian prisoners of war, for the Provisional Government, and for other objects of special concern. At the end of the service the Archbishop came from the altar behind the *ikonostas* and, standing at the chancel where the vast audience stood as close to him as possible, he preached to them a marvelous sermon. I was told, by one who understands the Russian language, that it was a model of pastoral eloquence. A large section of the sermon was devoted to telling the people about the Christians in America. He characterized, with aptness, what they have in common with the Russian Christians. He frankly admitted the differences, but insisted that they were all minor in contrast with the vital, essential points which unite us all. He ended by an appeal for Christian unity. Then there came a special prayer for the unity of all believers in accord with the prayer of our Lord.

Another opportunity of unique importance was that which came to me through an invitation to meet with the Commission appointed by the Holy Synod to Revise the Curriculum of the Ecclesiastical Academies and Seminaries. Among their number were leading professors and teachers of the institutions concerned, as well as of the universities, together with other educational authorities. I was asked not only to participate in the discussion but to give an address. It afforded me opportunity to point out recent developments and modern tendencies in theological education in America and Europe. Among the principal points which I developed, and which apparently had special and timely application to the needs in Russia were: The advantages of closer association of theological students and those of other faculties and callings; the desirability of extending the theological course or at least of making suitable provision for advanced studies; the combination, in proper proportions and with the wisest guidance, of practical experience in Christian service with the regular scholastic work; the giving of larger attention to those studies which prepare the future leaders of the Church to bring to bear the Christian Gospel on the social problems of our time; the preparation of church leaders for meeting the unparalleled missionary opportunity and responsibility of this generation; the furnishing of an apologetic calculated to enable the clergy to command the intellectual confidence and following of thoughtful unbelievers; the holding in true prominence of those studies and exercises which ensure vital Christian experience and true growth in spiritual apprehension and power. In the light of my study of the needs and requirements of the Russian priesthood, it would be difficult to indicate which of these points could wisely be omitted, or which of them needs chief emphasis. Considering the present political, social, economic, and religious problems of Russia, I would say that without hesitation, that by far the most critical is that which has to do with ensuring an able leadership of the Christian forces of the nation.

Much time was devoted to unhurried interviews with the recognized leaders of the Russian Church—metropolitans, archbishops, bishops, and clergymen, as well as professors, editors, and other intelligent and sympathetic laymen. I had eight extended visits of from two to five hours each with the High Procurator of the Holy Synod. He has proved to be the man for this difficult hour. He has the requisite background in knowledge of the Russian Church—its history, institutions, and genius. He has a vivid realization of the Church's recent lapses and present needs. He possesses the singleness of eye, the unselfish motive, the dauntless courage, the indifference to obstacles, and the dogged perseverance so necessary for dealing properly with the present large and difficult situation. It remains to be seen whether his constructive capacity is equal to the demands of this momentous year. I was encouraged by his open-mindedness and evident willingness and eagerness to receive advice. I discussed with him with the greatest fullness and particularity his plans and problems, and he repeatedly expressed his desire that I continue to keep in close touch with him. Here is a man who should be supported by the intercession of all well-wishers of the new Russia, for no one is in a position to do more to influence its destiny.

My relation to the religious life of Russia was not confined to my contacts with the Orthodox Church. I sought and improved opportunities to come into helpful touch with other religious bodies and movements. Never shall I forget the long evening spent with the Archbishop and the group of principal bishops of the largest dissenting sect—the Old Believers, who as already stated, number not less than twelve millions. This meeting was held in the simply furnished little log house of the Archbishop on the outskirts of Moscow. We gathered in a quiet room around one flickering candle, and talked late into the night about characteristics, persecutions, present-day problems and aspirations of this body of Christians who, by every test, have so well earned the right to be counted among Christ's true followers. These humble leaders showed their genuine gratitude and affection in a way that left a deep impression upon Mr. Crane and myself by bringing together on the following day from many of their churches their best singers and with this massed choir they had sung for us, with the unison and wonderful depth of religious fervor which characterize the singing of this sect, some fifteen of their most remarkable religious hymns, chants and prayers.

I met with the representatives of other Russian sects as I had opportunity. I also had most profitable conferences with representatives of the Protestant forces in Russia, notably with Dr. Keen of the British and Foreign Bible Society[42] and with

---

[42] The British and Foreign Bible Society, an interdenominational agency for the printing, distribution, and translation of the Bible, began working in Russia in the early nineteenth century and contributed to the translation of the Bible into contemporary Russian. William Keen served as an agent of the society in Russia from 1896 to 1918.

Dr. Simons of the Methodist Episcopal Church,[43] both of whom are conducting their work with great wisdom and evident acceptance. Memorable interviews were also had with the most distinguished and best trusted leaders of the seven millions of Russian and Polish Jews, which enabled me to penetrate more deeply than ever before into the heart of their problems. I am glad to believe that the Russian Revolution has at last ushered in a day of hope for these long-persecuted people. My conference with the Roman Catholic Bishop and with other representatives of that communion was likewise very satisfactory. One of the most memorable meetings which I had was with this Bishop and the High Procurator of the Holy Synod of the Orthodox Church. At the beginning of our conference I said: "Here we are, representatives of the three great Christian communions, Protestant, Roman Catholic, and Russian Orthodox. We have one Christ and one enemy. Though we differ on not a few points which each of us regards as vital, that which would unite us is so much more important that we should never cease to work and to pray that we may some day enter into the full unity which our Lord has had in view for all His disciples." They both responded with manifest sympathy to these words. We did not find it difficult, in the shadow of the tragedy of the great war and its overpowering sufferings, to find much ground for common action.

---

[43] The Methodist Episcopal Church began missionary work in Russia in the late nineteenth century. George A. Simons from the US served as a leader of the Methodist movement in Russia from 1908 until his departure in 1918.

ADDRESS OF JOHN R. MOTT, AT THE GREAT SOBOR OF THE RUSSIAN ORTHODOX CHURCH, MOSCOW, JUNE 19, 1917

Mr. President, and Members of the Great Sobor:

My friend, Mr. Crane, and I have been profoundly touched by your whole-souled welcome. We appreciate most sincerely the high honor you have conferred upon us in granting us the rare privilege of coming among you and of participating in your significant assembly. We have come in the name of the President and people of the United States of America. President Wilson in appointing a Special Mission to Russia consisting of our seven associates and ourselves and having at its head Senator Root, one of our most eminent American statesmen, charged us with the responsibility of conveying to the entire Russian nation the expression of the sympathy and good will of America at this momentous period of their history. We have recognized clearly that if our message is to reach the entire Russian nation and people it must be brought to the Russian Orthodox Church because we well know that your great Church constitutes indeed the heart of Russia.

Through all the years of the life of the American nation we have been bound to Russia by ties of friendship. They have been years of unbroken peace and of mutual helpfulness. The Russian Revolution with its triumph of democratic principles has established a new bond between these two great democracies. An even stronger bond was created when America decided to enter the world war and thus to identify herself with Russia in the great life and death struggle. What unity can be stronger than that which causes peoples to mingle for common ideals and purposes their very life blood? Just as the juices of the separate grapes are poured together under the pressure of the wine press so this titanic and unparalleled struggle which calls upon our two peoples to lay down on the altar of the world's liberty our best life blood will serve, as no other experience, to establish a deep and permanent unity between the Russian and American nations.

The best way in which we can voice our sense of appreciation of your welcome is to say quite simply and sincerely that we feel entirely at home as we come among you. It has been the privilege of both Mr. Crane and myself to maintain an intimate touch with many of the leaders and members of the various Eastern Churches. Only a few years ago while in the Levant I had the honor of meeting with the Patriarchs of Constantinople, Jerusalem, Alexandria, and Antioch[44] and also of visiting the ecclesiastical academies and theological seminaries on the Island of Halki, where through the kind arrangement of the Ecumenical Patriarch[45] I gave addresses to the students and professors, and also in Serbia, Bulgaria, Greece, and Egypt. We have likewise valued highly our frequent contacts with the Russian Orthodox Church. Such opportunities have presented themselves in our own country where your Church is so well established. In our different visits to Russia also we have enjoyed helpful fellowship with members of the Russian Church. Moreover, in my four visits to Japan I have always come into touch with the fruitful mission of your Church. On two of those visits I had the never-to-be-forgotten privilege of intimate association with that great Christian missionary and apostle, Archbishop Nicolai.[46] On one occasion he attended the Christian Student Conference which I was conducting and while there gave a most powerful address on how to bring the truth of Christ to the educated classes of Japan. On my last visit to that country I conducted a conference of the leaders of the Christian forces, and your own Bishop Sergius and also the head of your theological seminary were present as delegates. The opportunity of mingling with Russian Christians which I have appreciated most deeply was that which came to me during my two visits to the prisoner-of-war camps in Germany and Austria-Hungary. Possibly many of you do not know that the Christians of America early in the war were given permission to extend the helpful ministry of the Young Men's Christian Association to the prison camps of these countries and that we have had over thirty wise and unselfish American workers busily engaged throughout the larger part of the war in helping to meet the needs of the Russian prisoners as well as those of the other Allied countries. It would be difficult, yes impossible, to express to you adequately the sense of joy and deep satisfaction it has afforded us to be permitted in this way to become better acquainted with the Russian people and with the Russian soul. Anything which God will permit us to do directly or indirectly to serve the Russian prisoners we will gladly do.

There are three words or messages which I wish to bring to all the members of this Sobor and through you to the more than one hundred million men and women who belong to the Russian Orthodox Church. The first message I would convey is one of the deep gratitude of the American people to the Russian Christians and to the Russian people as a whole. We shall never forget the service rendered by Russia to our country at the time of our War for Independence and also again in the midst of our Civil War. Moreover, we recognize that in the present world war the Russian

---

[44] In Eastern Orthodox tradition, these four patriarchs hold the highest honorary roles of leadership.

[45] Ecumenical Patriarch is a title for the Patriarch of Constantinople (Istanbul).

[46] Archbishop Nikolai (Kasatkin, 1836–1912) established the first Orthodox church in Japan, where he served from 1861 to 1912.

soldiers and people have been fighting battles for us. I realize in some measure what a price you have paid on our behalf as well as your own in struggling for the freedom of the world, because I remember the two million lonely Russian prisoners so many of whom I have visited in the prisoner-of-war camps, also your hundreds of military hospitals which have at times been so crowded with suffering inmates; nor do I forget the countless graves and sorrowing homes. As we reflect on these sacrifices and sufferings is it strange that my people feel under a sense of lasting gratitude to Russia? We are also deeply grateful because of what you are proposing and planning to do to continue this struggle to a successful issue. That you will do this we do not question. Let me also mention as a ground for thankfulness to Russia the valuable constructive service accomplished within the United States by the Russian Orthodox Church. America is a cosmopolitan country. Among the people who have come to us from different lands are millions of Russians. What do we not owe to your Church in following them with its blessed ministries and helping to develop among them true Christian citizens. Never can we speak too highly of the splendid foundations laid by your Church leaders such as the highly beloved Archbishop Platon and Archbishop Tikhon. American Christians are likewise profoundly grateful to the Russian Church for all that it has done through the centuries to enrich our common Christianity. We think of your great contributions in the realm of ecclesiastical architecture and sacred art, through your noble and uplifting churches and cathedrals, through the wonderful frescoes and paintings and through the many priceless ikons. We have been profoundly moved by your Church music, a sphere in which you excel all other Christians. Here let me pay a tribute to my countryman and friend, Mr. Charles R. Crane, who through the years has had such a sympathetic interest in all that is best in Russian life. As some of you know, he was the means, through his large financial cooperation, of bringing over to America some of your best Church singers and of building up in connection with the Russian Cathedral in New York one of the best Russian Church choirs in the world. Its sacred concerts given among lovers of the best music in all our great cities, in our universities and at Christian gatherings have already accomplished much in the direction of cultivating among the Christians of America a love for the best Church music. One of your greatest contributions to the Christian religion has been your faithful and fearless witness through the centuries to great and essential Christian truths. With grateful memory we also recall the lives of many of your confessors, martyrs, and saints.

My second message is an expression of solicitude and sympathetic caution lest in this time of great upheaval the position and hold of the Russian Church be weakened. The foundations of the world are heaving. Institutions which we had thought solid and enduring have deprived to be resting on shifting sand. Christ and His Church were never so necessary, never so unique and, if given their central position, will prove never to have been more sufficient. None of us will forget that in the period of the Tartars[47] and in other times of grave menace it was the Russian Church which held the nation together. It has been most encouraging and inspiring to visit this great gathering and to see the open-minded and thorough way in which so many of your Church leaders are facing their problems and seeking to adapt the Church to new and modern conditions. This process is sure to result in a great and lasting good. Let us have the courage to welcome and accept the truth from any quarter. In this period of change and readjustment, while we are earnestly seeking to lay hold on new truth for the life and work of the Church, let us with like intensity and conviction hold fast to all that is true in historic Christianity; let us continue to ring true regarding the unchangeable and mighty truths of creedal Christianity; let us in a day of crass materialism and of cold intellectualism preserve the priceless possession of mystical Christianity; let us at all costs see that our Christianity is abounding in vitality; and, through the fearless and unflinching application of Christ's principles; let us insist that it be made an adequate transforming power in social and national life and in international relationships.

My third message is one of hope and reassurance. You are engaged in the greatest struggle which the world has ever known. I come to remind you that the United States is with you in this conflict to the very end. The American people love peace and hate war. We did all that we could do in justice to our conscience to keep out of this world war, but finally to be true to our souls and our highest guiding principles we found it necessary to join you and the other Allies. In doing so we have counted the cost and are ready to pay it. Since I left my home ten millions of American young men have registered themselves as ready to serve their nation in this struggle in any way which the authorities may designate. This great host is being called up in lots of five hundred thousand each to be thoroughly trained. The week I left America fourteen great officers' camps were opened in which over forty thousand officers are being prepared for their responsibilities. Our Congress has already authorized the raising through loans and taxation for war expenditures this first year the equivalent of over thirty-five billions of rubles. Our various states and municipalities as well as the national Government have thrown themselves with earnestness into the work of preparation. All our great industries are being mobilized with reference to rendering the maximum of service in the war. The work of production and distribution has been put in the ablest hands for the same purpose, and our means of communication have been placed at the disposal of the Government. General Pershing and some of the first contingent of our troops have landed in France. We already have naval vessels at work in European waters. It may safely be said that ninety-nine per cent, if not more, of the American people stand solidly behind our great President in the purposes which he has announced. Let this message, therefore, remind you that you are not alone. Go

---

[47] Here Mott is referring to the time after the Mongol invasion from the thirteenth to the fifteenth century, when eastern Slav leaders were required to pay tribute to Tatar khans.

back to all your parishes in cities, towns, and villages and tell the Russian people that America is with them. Say to them that just as Russia came to the help of America in the darkest hours of her history, so America now joins Russia in this moment of grave crisis. Tell them to stand firmly behind the Provisional Government. Tell them to be true to the Church that it may in this time of colossal strain preserve the solidarity of the nation. Tell them that we believe that, in view of what Russia has already achieved in this war, in view of the wonderful sacrifices which the Russian people have already made, in view of the vast and vital issues at stake, and in view of the urgency of the situation and the gravity of the crisis, Russia and her Allies must continue steadfast to the end. Above all let the Church be unfailing in reminding the people that God only can enable us to accomplish His high and holy purpose. While everything else is changeable and changing Jesus Christ "is the same yesterday, today, yea, and forever."

LETTER FROM THE HIGH PROCURATOR OF THE RUSSIAN ORTHODOX CHURCH TO JOHN R. MOTT

Chancellory of the High Procurator of the Holy Synod of Russia
Petrograd, July 6th, 1917.

My dear Sir,

The most kind and helpful conversations which you have had with me regarding the important affairs of the Orthodox Church in Russia evoked in my own heart a sense of sincere gratitude, especially for the brotherly appreciation and sympathy which you have manifested for my dear Mother Church. I trust and hope that in the future also you will not leave me without the help of your wise counsel and support as I seek to discharge the important responsibilities entrusted to me by the people. I am indeed grateful to you for your coming to Russia at this time. Your visit and the messages which you delivered at the Convention of the clergy and laity of all Russia in Moscow and before the Holy Synod and other leaders of the Church in Petrograd have shown us that your love for the Christian Church and your ability to perceive the truth of the Christian faith are true not only of yourself but also of those many lovable Christian hearts in America whom you have so well represented. May Our Lord bless you for your largeness of heart.

Regarding that part of your important letter in which you express the desire that the Russian Orthodox Church be represented officially at the proposed Conference on Faith and Order[48] to be held in America within a few years, I would say that I am profoundly interested in this Conference and respond with all my soul to its high aims as set forth by you in your communication. I believe that the plan of the Conference is wise in not making it a legislative body but limiting its work to that of bringing together for fellowship and interchange of knowledge and experience members of the various Christian Communions of the world. Such exchange of knowledge about the distinctive teachings, principles, forms of government, and work of the great

---

[48] The Faith and Order Movement grew out of the World Missionary Conference of 1910 in Edinburgh, which was chaired by Mott. The focus of the movement was the unity of the global church. The first World Conference on Faith and Order met in Lausanne, Switzerland, August 3–21, 1927.

Christian Churches will result in very great good. I assure you, therefore, that as High Procurator of the Holy Synod of the Russian Orthodox Church I will see, so far as it depends upon me, that suitable representatives of our Church are sent to the proposed Conference. I shall be glad to have you report this fact, and also would like to have you arrange to have sent to me all printed circulars and pamphlets which may be issued from time to time dealing with the plans for the Conference.

With profound respect for the great and useful work accomplished by the American Special Mission now in Russia, and for you my dear brother in Jesus Christ,

I beg to remain,
Faithfully yours,
VLADIMIR LVOV,[49]
High Procurator of the Holy Synod of Russia.

DR. JOHN R. MOTT,
Envoy Extraordinary of the United States of America on Special Mission to Russia, Winter Palace, Petrograd.

---

[49] Vladimir N. Lvov (1872–1930) served as ober-procurator of the Holy Synod from March 3 to July 24, 1917. He was replaced by Anton Kartashev.

Figure 1. Cyrus H. McCormick, Jr., and John R. Mott, summer 1917. Special Collections, Yale Divinity School Library.

Figure 2. Root Mission to Russia, summer 1917. Special Collections, Yale Divinity School Library.

Figure 3. The American Mission to Russia, summer 1917. Special Collections, Yale Divinity School Library. Standing from right to left: Major Stanley Washburn, assistant secretary to the mission; Basil Miles, secretary; Lieutenant Alva D. Bernhard, aide to Admiral Glennon; surgeon Holton S. Curl, USN; Hugh A. Moran; Brigadier General William V. Judson (detailed to remain in Petrograd as military attaché to the American embassy); Brigadier General R. E. L. Michie, aide to the chief of staff; Baron de Ramsay, attaché of the Russian Foreign Office; F. Willoughby Smith, assistant secretary and American consul at Tiflis; and Lieutenant Colonel T. Bentley Mott. Seated from right to left: Charles Edward Russell; Samuel R. Bertron; John R. Mott; Rear Admiral James H. Glennon; Ambassador David R. Francis; Elihu Root, chairman; Major General Hugh L. Scott, chief of staff; James Duncan; Charles R. Crane; and Cyrus H. McCormick.

Figure 4. Summer 1917. Special Collections, Yale Divinity School Library. From left to right: M. I. Terestchenko, Russian minister of foreign affairs; General Alexis Brusiloff, at the time commander in chief of the Russian army; Elihu Root, head of the American Mission to Russia; Major General Hugh L. Scott; and Brigadier General R. E. L. Michie, of the American army.

Figure 5. Members of the American Mission to Russia and the Board of Trade of Petrograd, summer 1917. Special Collections, Yale Divinity School Library.

SERVICE WITH FIGHTING MEN

AN ACCOUNT OF THE WORK OF THE AMERICAN YOUNG MEN'S CHRISTIAN ASSOCIATIONS IN THE WORLD WAR

Editorial Board

Chairman
WILLIAM HOWARD TAFT

Managing Editor
FREDERICK HARRIS

Associate Editors
FREDERIC HOUSTON KENT
WILLIAM J. NEWLIN

ASSOCIATION PRESS
New York: 347 Madison Avenue
1922

Chapter XLVIII
RUSSIA

The beginning of the work in Russia illustrates once more how essential was its reciprocal basis. Quite apart from the Association's own international standpoint, the situation was such that the service had to be for all prisoners or for none. Scarcely had the first experimental work commenced in Germany when Dr. Harte encountered a new obstacle to its extension.

"I have not had the freedom," states one of his letters, "that is needed really to help the 900,000 prisoners of war in Germany. In every official interview, I was asked what we were doing for the Germans in Russia."

German Policy

Since, at that time, the Germany policy was to congregate all the Allied prisoners in mixed camps, the Y service could not be confined to the British and French, and it soon became evident that the work already begun in Göttingen and elsewhere would be imperiled unless means could be found to enter the Russian field, where most of the captured Germans and Austrians were held. From the beginning of the war, the German nation was deeply concerned about the fate of their fellow countrymen in the hands of the Russians. Many wild stories of their sufferings in Siberia were current. Nothing too terrible could be imagined concerning those who were swallowed up in that vast, terrifying country of eternal snows, the land where so many political prisoners of the tsar had suffered and died. It is easy enough to understand this anxiety and to understand how Russia became the keystone of the arch that the Y was striving to build.

Accordingly Dr. Harte in May, 1915, left Berlin for Petrograd to advocate extending the War Prisoners' Aid in this new sphere.

The Y Enters Russia

For two weeks after his arrival in Petrograd, Dr. Harte was busy in securing the interest of influential persons, notably the Assistant Minister of Foreign Affairs, the

Procurator of the Holy Synod, the Empress, the Dowager Empress, and the British and American Ambassadors. In early June he was finally able to secure permission to visit the prison camps in Siberia, and set out accompanied by one of the YMCA secretaries. His report of this tour with its favorable tone and its entirely sympathetic and constructive suggestions had much to do with resolving Russian doubts and Russian sensitiveness to outside interference in her own responsibilities; so that on June 14th he was able to report official permission to establish YMCA service with two secretaries. A modest beginning was made at once at Moscow and at Kiev—the latter the point at which were entrained the thousands of captives sent into the Siberian expanse. By the end of August, American friends had enabled Dr. Mott to authorize the program for an extensive Russian service.

Concessions in Germany

Dr. Harte now went back to Berlin, to return to Petrograd in October bringing good news of further concessions in Germany. He carried with him three immense sacks of letters and post-cards to their Russian relations and friends from Russian war prisoners in Germany and boxes of gifts to prisoners in Russia from their relatives, a consignment of musical instruments and numerous other articles. Better still, he was able to take with him a Russian prisoner. This man, the nephew of a prominent official in Russia, was an officer who had lost a leg; and, in personal appreciation of Dr. Harte's services, the head of the German War Prisoners' Department turned him over to the Y representative in order to facilitate his work in Russia. In return, Dr. Harte secured an invalided German prisoner who was sent back to Germany. At once the Russians responded generously to the suggestion of reciprocity, so that Dr. Harte cabled to America for eight American secretaries to take charge of eight provincial centers with a main office in Petrograd—this in addition to the two secretaries already on the ground. Dr. Harte had also brought with him 150,000 marks from Germany for prisoner relief and 100,000 marks from Austria, and had available 120,000 marks from America. He now made another trip to Vladivostok and on his return reported the formation of a strong committee of distinguished Russians authorized to give official and legal standing to the work of the War Prisoners' Aid. As in other countries, this committee acted as a clearing house for all services between Germany and her nationals in Russia, and Russia and her nationals in Germany.

The work in Russia was somewhat slow in gaining headway because of the extreme difficulty of getting suitable men in America willing and able to carry it on. By March, 1916, however, there were six secretaries, and by the end of the year, nineteen. The central office was at Petrograd and the men visited camps in the provinces and governments of Irkutsk, Kazan, Yeniseysk, Zabaikal, Tomsk,

Akmolinsk,[1] Bukhara, Fergana, Kiev, Orenburg, Perm, Primorsk, Primorskaya, Samara, Samarkand, Simbirsk,[2] Syr-Darjinksaya, Tobolsk, Tschernigorak, and Zakaspdeskaya.[3] Hampered as they were by geographical, political, and especially language factors, they represented the only disinterested agency for the alleviation of the lot of about 500,000 German and Austrian prisoners of war then scattered through some 70 Russian and Siberian camps.

What the Y Faced

The Ground to be Covered

Let the reader bear in mind, however, that this was but a small part of the total number of war prisoners. What that number was we cannot be sure;[4] but we do know that in May, 1917, the number of camps which could be visited by the small force of American secretaries was 68 out of a total of 891—771 in Russia and 120 in Siberia; and that of these 68 but 52 were reported to have been effectively reached by the Association. Add to this the fact that every secretary had a territory many times the size of Great Britain—Turkestan, for instance, with 30 camps, having an area 16 times that of England; that these huge territories were in many cases inadequately provided with railway facilities, so that sometimes long journeys had to be made by horseback or sledge; that the interminable Siberian winter further curtailed travel and with the darkening of days must inevitably have darkened the spirits of the exiled war prisoners; that in many camps little attempt at sanitation could be made with insufficient water even to wash hands and faces, no soap or towels, clothing so scanty that barracks could not possibly be ventilated and a man could not wash his shirt without freezing in the process; that in such camps the men were without exception infested with lice and vermin, the sick lying among the healthy—advanced cases of tuberculosis included—the latrines in disgusting condition, and epidemics an ever present menace; that the Russian soldiers lived in much the same way and the military authorities resented any determined effort to introduce new methods on a large scale; that food was poor and medical supplies scarce—add these factors, and it

---

[1] Today Nur-Sultan, Kazakhstan.

[2] Today Ulyanovsk, Russia.

[3] This edition includes updated spelling for several place names if current spellings were able to be found. The original text from William Howard Taft, et al., eds., *Service with Fighting Men: An Account of the Work of the American Young Men's Christian Associations in the World War*, volume 2 (New York: Association Press, 1924) includes two attached fold-out maps which mark the locations of many sites of YMCA activities in Russia.

[4] [Footnote in original text] Estimates place the total figure at 1,250,000 to 1,500,000.

becomes evident that, with the meager personnel the Y could command, the problem of adequately caring for prisoners in Russia and Siberia was intrinsically impossible of solution. Large as the ultimate achievement appears in its totality, the surface only could be scratched.

What Russia Accomplished

This is not to say that Russia failed to comprehend the problem herself. On the contrary, Dr. Harte's report of his first trip through the camps, even taking into account the fact that he was purposely writing of the good that he saw and not the bad, shows that they had accomplished much. Most of the difficulties outlined above are the physical and geographical, or represent psychological factors that have grown through centuries of tsardom and bureaucracy with its peculiar attitude toward the masses wrought of sentimental paternalism and hard contempt. At the same time, undoubtedly an outstanding characteristic of the Russian is compassion, a singularly acute understanding of the human heart and its needs; and through all the bureaucratic inefficiency, through all the insurmountable physical difficulties, this compassion sent its fine influence carrying a certain balm for imprisoned men. All those Russians who understood—and they were many in high places and low—did much for the prisoners.

In Siberian Villages

The facts that bear this out are among the most picturesque in war prisoner history. In the early days, for example, Russia sent her prisoners to remote Siberian villages. Here they were quartered among the villagers or assigned separate houses as dwellings. The freedom of the village was theirs, and the peasants treated them as sons and brothers. They shopped in the village shop and brought milk and cream and fresh eggs, honey and butter and vegetables from the peasants' wives; they bathed and swam in the river, and they lounged and told tales under the trees. They received 21 kopecks a day, or 80 kopecks if they worked in the fields and forests. Sometimes, near large towns, the municipality employed prisoners on public works as at Tomsk where they were engaged in building new and higher banks as for the river, and in the words of Dr. Harte, "enjoy the freedom, the fresh air, the river baths, and the good food and work somewhat leisurely." In the towns, too, many prisoners were employed by the bakers, confectioners, tailors, and cabinet-makers, and were paid accordingly. Often such prisoners lived freely in the city and were considerately treated on the streets and in public buildings. Musicians were especially favored; instruments were furnished them, and they were paid for giving concerts in nearby towns.

This habit of treating prisoners as the Russian soldiers themselves were treated extended as well to the hospitals. Again and again during his first tour Dr. Harte remarked that in handling the wounded and ill everything was forgotten except their needs and everything possible was done for their comfort and safe recovery. Russian soldiers and German prisoners lay side by side on the cots, receiving the same zealous attention from doctors and nurses. In the larger centers especially, the hospitals were clean, light, roomy, and efficient. In passing, it may be noted that many of them had been vodka warehouses.

Concentration Camps

Subsequently, however, Russia adopted the concentration-camp plan of the other warring countries, erecting camps to house 10,000 men each—a process that was going on at the time of Dr. Harte's first visit. But even here, prisoners seemed to have been treated on the same basis as Russian soldiers, housed in the same barracks, given the same food—a fact that implied equally bad conditions as well as equally good, it should be noted. In many camps, nevertheless, things were in astonishingly good shape, all factors considered. Welfare work was under way, music and recreation were encouraged, and above all the officers were patient, harbored no enmity, and worked hard in the interests of the men.

The Work of the Y

The Y secretaries were assigned to various military districts and governments, generally immense distances apart, with a central office at Petrograd to serve as directive agency, distribution point, and clearing house. There were two broad types of supervision: one where the secretary had many camps to visit and had to devote considerable time to traveling, the other where he was located at one camp or spent his time between two or three. As elsewhere, the work in the camps was of the community type, aiming to develop the maximum of activity and volunteer service with the minimum of equipment and expense. For this reason, a large share of the responsibility was handed over to the camp associations, organized by the Y secretaries and operating through an efficient system of committees. By intensive work at the start, even the traveling secretaries were able to develop strong associations in camps which they could visit for only a few hours once every month or two. The plan of organization followed in the Irkutsk Military District will serve as a model. It included an Executive Committee, and committees directing activities of welfare, school, religion, music, library, and camp beautification.

Buildings and Equipment

In Russia, it was not, as in other countries, necessary for the Y to build special huts. Only four of these, in fact, were erected; in most camps permission was readily obtained to take over vacated barracks, with a large resultant saving in energy, time, and money. These barracks were adapted, attractively decorated, and furnished by the Association. Partitions, often movable, were erected by the prisoners to divide them into kitchens, buffets, class rooms, lecture halls, reception rooms, churches, reading rooms, music rooms, and shops. Sometimes, starting with a single room, the Y was able to take over in the same camp two, three, four, or more entire barracks.

Specific Activities

Much of the Y work, of course, consisted of exactly the same elements as in other warring countries. There were the recreational features—doubly necessary to the morale of the men during the long Siberian winter nights—consisting of games, plays, and operettas, for which both encouragement and material were supplied by the Y; the same indoor gymnastics and outdoor athletics,[5] with skating an especially popular feature in winter and tennis in the summer; the same cultivation of vegetable and flower gardens, the same garden contests. As many of these activities, however, have features peculiar to their environment, it is necessary to describe some of them in greater detail to give an adequate picture of the Russian situation. It should be remembered throughout that the work of the Y was, as it were, intensified and broadened in Russia because of the fact that it was the only organization permitted within the camps, so that it became the agent for numerous other organizations. Whatever was done for the prisoners in Russia was perforce done through the YMCA.

Libraries

During the first year of imprisonment before the YMCA began its activities the scarcity of reading material in the Russian prison camps was appalling. At Voenny Gorodok, for instance, when the educational work was begun in November, 1915, with 1,700 students and 35 teachers, but 15 textbooks could be secured. At Darnitza an American secretary reports bringing out a dozen language textbooks and a score of dictionaries, the only books he happened to have on hand, for the entertainment of some 1,500 prisoner officers about to be entrained; he was as swamped with demands for them as though they had been popular novels. The solution of the problem of

---

[5] [Footnote in original text] At Beresovka during the winter of 1916–1917 three skating places were maintained. After the ice had broken, there were playing daily at this camp 25 football teams, 50 volley-ball teams, and 10 teams of baseball or rounders. Naturally this activity had a large effect for good on the health and vitality of the participants.

securing books was long and difficult. The bookstores in Moscow and Petrograd were ransacked for everything that could in any way serve the prisoners, and books were bought from private citizens. The problems of censorship and transportation had to be dealt with in turn. Finally, with the cooperation of the Danish Book Commission, which was able to secure a large supply of books from Denmark, the situation was relieved. By the winter of 1916–1917 at least fifty libraries had been established containing from 100 to 4,000 volumes each, every library under the supervision of a competent librarian selected by the prisoners, and the majority of the libraries equipped with a book bindery. A special book department was added to the office at Petrograd in November, 1916. This had much to do with the efficient handling of the library problem. In addition to the libraries, hundreds of individual orders for books were received from prisoners and filled wherever possible, some coming from camps which were not visited by secretaries. Among the larger libraries were those at Omsk, with 533 volumes, Peschanka with 1,444, Tomsk with 500, and Orenburg with 1,500. There were libraries in fifteen of the sixteen camps of the Irkutsk military district. What these libraries meant may be judged from the fact that in one of those in the Irkutsk district which opened for the drawing of books at 10 a.m., there were 20 to 50 men in line by 9.30 to make sure of a book, and every book was drawn every day, to be returned the same evening. Books in Russian were also furnished by the Y for the Russian guards, who appreciated them no less than the prisoners.

Schools

One of the most remarkable features of the war prisoners' work in Russia was the development of educational activities. In the year preceding May, 1917, there were at least 31 organized schools in 30 different camps, with an enrollment of over 20,000 students taught by more than 1,000 different teachers practically all of whom were prisoners, many being well-known university professors, writers, lawyers, business and professional men. At Voenny Gorodok, within three weeks after the arrival of the secretary, there was a full-fledged "university" in operation with 1,700 students, 35 teachers, and 27 courses, and with classes running every hour of the day from 8 a.m. until 9 p.m. At Tomsk there were 54 classes taking 23 different subjects; at Krasnoyarsk, 652 students, 25 courses, and classes from 7 a.m. to 8 p.m.; at Beresovka, 2,500 students and 60 teachers. Language studies predominated, then commercial subjects followed by legal, professional, cultural, and artistic branches. These classes were conducted in German, Hungarian, Czech, Ukrainian, Italian, Polish, Hebrew, Croatian, Serbian, and Romanian. In one camp the teachers, unable to secure a primer, wrote one by hand and copied it on an improvised hectograph; these men had set as their ideal that no one willing to work should go home unable to read and write. At another camp, nine out of every ten officers learned or perfected one or more foreign languages during a period of eight months, and every German soldier in the camp was enrolled in an English class.

Music

From the beginning, an especially important activity of the YMCA in Russian and Siberian prison camps was the organization and assisting of orchestras, choirs, and choruses. Several factors brought this about: the positive craving of German, Austrian, and especially Hungarian prisoners for music, which was as necessary to their daily lives as food; the natural musical talent of these peoples and the presence among them of distinguished directors and musicians of the Central Empires, especially among those from Vienna and Budapest; and the bent for music of the Russian authorities themselves, who looked with especial favor on this form of activity and often organized their own orchestras. In May, 1917, orchestras had been reported from 31 camps, with between 700 and 800 instruments in regular use, and there were choirs and choruses in practically as many camps—in many cases both German and Hungarian choruses. The activities of these musical organizations were largely concerts during the week, assisting with Sunday services, and providing entertainment for the hospitals. In numerous cases where a sufficient number of musical instruments could not be purchased or were not donated, those needed were made by the prisoners themselves. "I know not how many unfortunate Siberian horses," wrote one secretary, "sacrificed their tails for (violin) bows." In other cases, too, musical compositions could not be secured, and whole song-books were written down laboriously from memory. A Hungarian officer at Orenburg startled the camp by writing Schubert's Mass from memory in preparation for the first Catholic service; later he made complete orchestrations for music the Y could secure for voice and piano only. Several prisoners wrote original solo, orchestral, and even light operatic compositions which were publicly produced in the camp. One camp had two orchestras—one of 45 instruments—a stringed orchestra, a German maennerchor[6] of 40 voices, and a Hungarian maennerchor of 38 voices.

Workshops and Factories

Although in some camps workshops had been started before the arrival of the Y, in many nothing of this kind had been done; and the Association at once organized carpenter shops, shoe shops, book-binderies especially needed to repair the well-thumbed library volumes—wood-carving departments, tailor shops, blacksmith shops, basket-making shops, paint shops, and arts-and-crafts departments. In Russia, the War Prisoners' Aid was particularly successful in combining work of this kind

---

[6] Men's chorus.

with relief work, this helping to solve two problems at once as well as training men to a future life of wider usefulness. At Orenburg, for example, the shoe department repaired 1,300 pairs of shoes and made 300 new pairs. The tailoring shop, housed in two rooms, turned out several thousand garments a month, made partly from materials supplied by the Red Cross but mostly from old clothes cast off by men who were fortunate enough to receive new clothing. Two old overcoats would be remade into one good one. Every scrap of cloth was saved to be made up into puttees.[7]

One particularly noteworthy development of this work was that completely equipped factories were established under the auspices of the Association, at Krasnoyarsk and several other places. This development was forced by the growing scarcity of soap and of leather. The soap factory was the first venture, and it soon supplied not only the camp laundry but also the Russian camp authorities with all the laundry soap they required, and had branched out into the manufacture of toilet soap, disinfecting soap, and shoe polish. Next a tannery was opened. By January, 1917, it was turning out excellent sole leather and uppers of horse hide, calf, and sheep skin, and was using about 800 hides per month. All the leather thus produced by the prisoners went to supply the needs of the various internment camps.

Convalescent Kitchens

An illuminating example of the ingenuity employed in enhancing the value of help from other agencies is seen in the invalid food kitchens established by the Y in the Yeniseysk, Irkutsk, and Transbaikal Provinces, and at Orenburg and Tomsk. These kitchens, intended for prisoners who were weak, invalid, or convalescent, had a capacity each of from 100 to 2,200 meals a day, and were run on a self-supporting plan which at the same time permitted those who had no money to obtain meals free. In March, 1917, for example, a train-load of dried fruits, sugar, rice, and beans forwarded by the American Red Cross was received by the American Embassy and turned over to the Y for distribution. This food was then purchased by the kitchen committees of the various camps from the camp executive committees at a moderate valuation, the kitchen committees in turn reimbursing themselves by issuing tickets for each meal to prisoners at, say, a half-kopeck each over the cost. Both the half-kopeck profit—which in three weeks might amount to enough for the purchase of 75 meals—and the entire amount received in the first instance by the executive committees would then be used to purchase meal tickets for those sans kopecks of their own. A per capita allowance was also made by which the officers could purchase part of the provisions at the same price, this money likewise going into meal tickets for the penniless. At Verkhne-Udinsk[8] more than 66,300 meals were thus provided up to

---

[7] Leg wrappings worn by soldiers.

[8] Today Ulan-Ude, Russia.

the end of 1916; at Peschanka, about 160,000 by the end of April, 1917. In 1916–1917 more than 5,000 per day were served from all these kitchens, and the average cost of the meals was 20–27 kopecks (13 to 18 cents). With food conditions as bad as they were in Russia at this time, it is impossible to estimate how many lives were saved by this additional nourishment furnished just where it was needed most. A Russian general who had seen something of the work at Peschanka said that he would like the Y to establish similar kitchens in every camp; and the German government appreciated the effort so thoroughly that they offered to continue their monthly contribution even after America had become an enemy nation.

Baths, Laundries, Barber, and Dental Services

In view of the evil conditions as regards cleanliness in many districts, with the constant risk of the introduction and spread of ravaging epidemics, the Y did what it could to supply bathing and laundry facilities. The need may be judged from the fact that at Orenburg, where water for bathing and washing had at first been carried by hand, the new clean, warm baths and laundries with piped water, installed by the Y, were frankly more deeply appreciated even than the hut. Barber shops also were organized in numerous camps. One of the most important services rendered was the supplementing of the wretched dental facilities and the complete installation in many cases of adequate dental equipment and offices, with the consequent relief of thousands of sufferers.

Religion

The YMCA in Russia and Siberia encouraged religious services impartially for all creeds and denominations. Rooms were equipped for the services of Greek Catholics, Roman Catholics, Protestants, Jews, and Mohammedans, the various articles used in the rituals, as well as Testaments and copies of the Koran being furnished by or through the Y; pastors and priests to conduct services were found among prisoners themselves, or in the cities without. Music was a highly prized accompaniment to these devotional exercises. In addition to the services of various creeds, there were, of course, many Bible study classes, the secretaries sometimes being compelled to write their own courses because of the shortage of books. As one chairman of a camp committee remarked:

> You know many of us back home before the War had gotten out of the habit of Bible reading; but now we feel the need for the book and are hungry for it. Many a man will read the book for the first time in years with an earnest endeavor to understand and apply it.

At Orenburg

A typical report of this many-sided religious work comes from Orenburg:

> We were fortunately located, since in this city of Orenburg lived Orthodox priests, a Lutheran pastor, rabbis, two Roman Catholic and several Mohammedan priests. Services have been held for all. The singing was always attractive, and the meetings, which were held outdoors during the warm weather, were attended by the majority of those interned in the camp. I shall never forget our first service, which was held early in July. I visited the priest several times, hoping to get his consent to come, but, as I could not guarantee him an undefiled building, it was hard to get the desired promise. We finally compromised on an open-air meeting. I had an organ sent in from the city and persuaded a fine old Polish count to make the necessary preparations. On the morning of the Mass, when we arrived, we were astonished to find that a high, attractive, evergreen altar, decorated with flowers and icons, had been erected against the stone wall of the prison. The priest's face fairly glowed, and it certainly was a beautiful sight. To this we added holy pictures, candles, silver altar cloth, communion service, a gold cross, etc. During the confession and communion service the men sat with staring eyes and seemed to be strangely touched. When the white-robed priest turned to begin the opening chant of the Mass, old and young sat with fixed faces, while the tears coursed down their cheeks as if, after two years' absence, it was too much for them.
>
> When the holy days of the Turks arrived, I hunted out a rich Tatar in the city and had him get a Koran and necessary holy food for our Mohammedan friends. We secured the church within the enclosure for them that they might pray to Allah and carry out their devotions as desired by the priest.
>
> We secured religious books and pamphlets for the Jews and took the men into the city under guard when their holy days arrived. Until the Czechs and Poles were removed to other lagers, we held Orthodox services for them regularly in the Greek church within the enclosure.

Individual Relief

Most of the enormous volume of individual relief and welfare work—much of it necessitated by the fact that the Y acted as agent in the camps for the Red Cross societies, the Embassies, and other organizations—was carried on in close cooperation with the camp welfare committees composed of prisoners. The Y secretary usually went to a camp loaded with money remittances for prisoners, gifts, food parcels, and clothing from relatives and other relief agencies to distribute, inquiries and replies to inquiries which had been forwarded from the Petrograd office; and this mass of material he turned over to the welfare committee to attend to and report on at his next visit. The welfare committees, under the direction of the secretaries, thus became the recognized agencies for the distribution of financial and other gifts where they would do the most good. As early as April, 1917, nearly 300 parcels a week were passing through the Petrograd office, more than 3,000 inquiries concerning prisoners being dealt with, more than 11,000 rubles a month being received for transmission to individuals. The list of such services, including the execution of the last wishes of the dying, the marking of graves, the procuring of books for special students, the changing of money, the arranging of marriages by proxy between distant sweethearts, the giving of a few rubles to thousands of soldiers setting out penniless for a long journey across the steppes—these could be extended to the length of Homer's catalog of ships.[9] No statistics would tell what they meant to lonely and depressed captives.

Post and Information Bureau

One feature of this work deserves special mention. At the beginning it became evident that some organized effort must be made to overcome the many difficulties in locating missing men, and forwarding mail, money, and parcels. With the hearty approval of the Chief of Staff, a central Post and Information Bureau was established at Irkutsk for the entire district, with an enormous card catalog of names and addresses, on which 48 men were employed. Subsequently, on proving its value and efficiency the bureau was taken over by the General Staff of Irkutsk and maintained as the center for the sixteen smaller local bureaus.

Disorganization and Reorganization

Early in 1917 came the American break with Germany and the consequent demand from the latter country that American Y secretaries in all fields be replaced by neutrals. In Russia, this was an especially difficult task; it had been difficult enough to secure the American secretaries in the first instance. The demand, too, came just at the time when Dr. Harte was advising the reduction of expenditures for recreation and diversion in view of the increasingly poignant need for such elementary necessities as food and surgical dressings. In the face of repeated demands from Germany in April and May for the withdrawal of Americans, therefore, the Americans still hung on and as late as mid-July those who were still at their posts had determined not to abandon their work unless forced to do so by the American Government itself; the need, they felt, was so desperately urgent. Meanwhile, however, the replacement by

---

[9] This expression refers to Book 2 of *The Iliad*, in which Homer presents a long list of Greek ships bound for Troy.

neutral secretaries from Denmark and Sweden had been going on gradually, and as rapidly as they were relieved the Americans were transferred to service for the Russian soldiers.

The Bolshevik Revolution

Then, in October, 1917, came the Bolshevik Revolution as a further disrupting influence. It did not immediately affect the work of the War Prisoners' Aid except for troublesome investigations by the Soviet authorities; but as the revolution spread, many camps were thrown open and a general unorganized exodus began toward Petrograd and Moscow. The work was now considered to be finished except for the salvaging of property, when suddenly a new situation arose with the Czechoslovak uprising, which cut off all rail communication with Siberia. In this situation the need for the Y was greater than ever, for the prisoners had been worked up into a fever of expectancy by the Brest-Litovsk Treaty and were in despair over this new obstacle to their early release.

So once again the Association took up its burden. Secretaries were sent into Siberia and the work went on until well into 1919. These neutral secretaries braved the dangers of Russia in the throes of revolution. For months they were cut off from communication with Petrograd. Some of them were arrested by the Soviet authorities and were in grave danger; but they continued to work as long as possible and always to the extent of their ability. At Orenburg the factory system was extended and became self-supporting. In twenty-five camps visitation was maintained. But it was heartbreaking labor since these secretaries were continually hampered by the Bolsheviks, by the lack of transport and communication, and by the frequent movement of the prisoners from camp to camp. What remained of the work was finally turned over to the German and Austrian Commissions.

Chapter LVIII
WARTIME ACTIVITIES IN RUSSIA

The story of the Association's wartime activities in Russia reflects the social maelstrom in which it had its setting. It is an epic of individuals laboring under adverse political, economic, and military conditions in the breakdown and smashup of that once mighty empire.

Always the immense geographical extent of European and Asiatic Russia must be kept in mind. Service points were scattered from the Arctic Ocean to the Black Sea, from Romania to the Pacific. Limitations of narrative space force the grouping in a single paragraph of Tashkent and Irkutsk, cities farther apart than New York and Denver. Secretaries accompanied the Czechoslovaks in their anabasis[10] from Kiev to Vladivostok, a distance of more than 6,000 miles, and then recrossed Siberia three or four times with those enthusiastic pro-Allies fighting to keep open the Trans-Siberian Railway. Frequent reference to the map is essential, therefore, to comprehension of the story.

Revolutionary Conditions

Political events made a kaleidoscopic background. The Russian Revolution occurred March 11, 1917. Less than a month later, the United States entered the war. The first effect of this was the forced withdrawal, at Germany's insistence, of Americans working with prisoners of war in the Russian camps. These secretaries then started a short-lived work for Russian soldiers at widely separated points.

After recognition of the Kerensky Government, the United States, in June 1917, sent a mission to Russia headed by Elihu Root. Dr. John R. Mott was a member. Through his activity, arrangements were made to start welfare work on a large scale with the Russian Army. By successive acts the Kerensky Government granted larger privileges than any other Government had afforded to the Association. Strenuous efforts were made to recruit more workers in America.

When some 50 of these arrived the next fall they found that the Bolshevik Revolution of November 7th had seriously altered the situation. The Soviet Government was anxious for a general peace and was about to make a separate

---

[10] A long military expedition in reference to the fourth-century BC work by Xenophon.

peace with the Central Powers. Soldiers had abandoned the front in great numbers. Workers stayed with the troops on sufferance and the position of Americans intent on war work was almost untenable. Some went home, others entered the service of the U.S. Government. The rest retired to Samara for conference. Army work was out of the question for the time being. Those who remained engaged in civilian relief work, city or rural, or in service for prisoners. This condition continued from March until September, 1918.

Meanwhile a great change was preparing. In July and August, 1918, Allied troops, including an American force, were sent to Murmansk and Archangelsk. In August, the United States Government announced its intention of cooperating with Japan in military support of the Czechoslovaks, in keeping open the Trans-Siberian Railway, and in protection of war materials at Vladivostok. This intervention constituted an international complication which forced the ultimate withdrawal of all Americans from Soviet Russia. Thenceforward the work was with the various Allied units and with civilians in Siberia and North Russia.

A Difficult Position

Seldom, if ever, has the Association found itself in a more difficult position. It was, of course, enthusiastically loyal to the Allied cause yet, on principle, desired to abstain from all partisanship in the midst of a welter of parties. This very non-partisanship made all partisans suspicious, and it is remarkable that the secretaries suffered no more than they did from the inevitable resentment aroused in many Russians by Allied intervention.

The story thus divides itself into periods corresponding to the successive political situations. First came scattered and short-lived attempts under the provisional government; then vigorous but quickly frustrated efforts, extending into the Soviet regime, to sustain the morale of the Revolutionary Army; then an interlude of civilian and relief work; finally, Allied intervention set a new task with distinct fields of work.

Measured by the huge bulk of seething Russia, the total achievement was not large. Considering the conditions, and comparing the number of workers to the millions to be served, the efforts appear as substantial achievements. The first aim—to help Russian fighting men in the war—could not be attained. The second—to make easier the hard life of thousands of soldiers in Arctic snows and on Siberian steppes and to relieve civilian distress—was successful so far as conditions permitted. The ultimate hope awaits fulfillment—that a demonstration of human fellowship and American helpfulness might restore or inspire in some Russians a faith now submerged by the hates, fears, ambitions and cruelties of war, and so aid them in finding the way to an ordered peaceful life.

Welfare Work Before the Summer of 1917

The "Lighthouse" in Petrograd

In 1900 there had been founded in Petrograd, the *Mayak*, or "Lighthouse," under the direction of Franklin A. Gaylord, with the aid of some other American secretaries, generously supported by James Stokes of New York. This was virtually a city Association on the American model with a membership of several thousand. It was a local organization, which did not adopt the Paris basis and become officially a Young Men's Christian Association until the winter of 1917.

The only other group of American secretaries in Russia was an organization of ten to fifteen men especially recruited in the United States for the work of the War Prisoners' Aid. Their headquarters were in Petrograd, but their service points were at the prisoner camps in places as widely separated as Petrograd, Kazan, Orenburg, Tashkent, Omsk, Tomsk, Irkutsk, and Chita. In these towns they promoted, in addition to work for prisoners, the organization of soldiers' clubs on a small scale, cooperating with committees of Russian officers and men, or with civilian committees of the Zemstvos. In the spring of 1917, requests came from several regiments for the establishment of clubs. When the United States became a belligerent, Germany insisted that Americans should cease work among prisoners of the Central Powers. Then the secretaries gave their whole attention to Russian soldiers' clubs. The undertakings ended with the recall of all secretaries to Moscow in the summer of 1917.

Turkestan

The American secretary of the War Prisoners' Aid in Turkestan shortly after his arrival perceived the possibility of YMCA work for Russian soldiers. After a period of unsuccessful effort on January 15, 1917, General Kuropatkin, Governor-General of Turkestan, gave permission to start specimen work in the Second Siberian Regiment at Tashkent.

Very shortly a large barrack was secured for moving pictures, lectures, and concerts. Movies were given three evenings a week with an attendance of over a thousand, a balalaika orchestra was organized and instruments provided. There were amateur theatricals, officers and soldiers working together. Special entertainments were given for units leaving for the front. On the first Sunday in April a reading and tea room was opened officially in the presence of representatives of the Army and the Church. This little club had a daily attendance of several hundred. Athletic and educational work was started and religious work was conducted in cooperation with the Orthodox chaplain of the regiment. Gifts of musical instruments, books, and writing materials were made to regiments going to the front. This work had the full cooperation of the Russian soldier committees and the general public.

Shortly afterwards permission was granted to work with the First Siberian Regiment at Troitzkoe, an isolated spot some thirty miles from the railroad. Even before the revolution, a moving picture machine was installed there, and classes in reading and writing and other activities were started. Later a reading and tea room was opened and the educational and athletic activities increased.

This work was on the way to a large expansion when the Y secretary was called to Petrograd in June, 1917. The work left in the hands of the Russian committees did not last long. Especially interesting and significant is the enthusiasm that these activities stimulated in Russian officers and soldiers, who cooperated in it even before the revolution of March 11, 1917. Compared with the difficulties encountered later, the accounts of these short-lived attempts read like the record of an earlier, happier time, a period of great hopes—destined, however, to cruel disappointment.

Peter and Paul Fortress, Petrograd

About the same time, work of a similar character was being started for the garrison of the Fortress of Peter and Paul, Petrograd, the *Mayak* secretaries cooperating with the Prisoners' Aid workers. On March 5, 1917, permission was granted to open a tea room. Classes and lectures were started then, and after Easter were well organized. Later a library of several thousand books was collected and frequent lectures were given. In May, 1917, 69 classes were in session, meeting three times a week for two hours each. Lectures on agricultural subjects were well attended and the daily count in the tea room was several hundred. When the Americans left Petrograd in the fall of 1918, this work was continued by Russian secretaries. After August, it was reported that the *Mayak* had been nationalized by the new officials, with the same Russian staff in charge.

Extension of Service

Work of a similar character was undertaken in the Kazan military district. An American secretary arrived in Kazan April 27, 1917, and tried to secure permits for the work, which was hardly started when the secretary was recalled to Moscow. Another secretary arrived in Orenburg in the spring of 1917 to start work of the same character. By June he had ten tents established for letter writing, and an athletic field and schools in operation. Further east along the line of the Trans-Siberian Railway were found early attempts at the same sort of work. A Y secretary in charge of war prisoners' work in Tomsk found local Russians interested and started work for soldiers in April and May, 1917. After much persistence in overcoming the idea that he might be engaged in anti-socialistic propaganda, he won their confidence and was able to direct activities. There was an auditorium and an athletic field. On June 4, 1917, the first baseball game was played. The secretary got a Russian carpenter to turn out some bats and bases. The bats resembled canoe paddles, and the bases milking stools; but by shortening the legs of the bases and driving them into the ground, they were made to serve, and some novel, if not strictly official, games of baseball followed.

Official Attitude

In June, 1917, the secretary of the War Prisoners' Aid in the Omsk military district found great interest in the work for Russian soldiers, but there is no record of activities getting started under his direction at this time. The essential point in reference to this matter is the kindly attitude of official classes towards the work of the YMCA and the general desire and willingness of various groups to cooperate. Still further east in Irkutsk and Chita, service to Russian soldiers was undertaken somewhat earlier and with better results, under the direction of the secretary of the War Prisoners' Aid for the Transbaikalia Military district. Unlike the instances reviewed above, this kept on during the summer of 1917 and was only interrupted by the Bolshevik movement of the fall and winter. Much of the most successful work here was of an athletic character. A large area for athletics had been provided in the main square of the city and American sports became very popular. The Cossacks did not always understand American ways. Their idea of playing volley ball was to slash at the ball with their swords. When a difference of opinion arose in football, instead of resorting to slugging, they chased each other around the field, brandishing their trusty swords. The populace invaded the field and held a political meeting which for a time broke up the athletic meet. They were especially nonchalant about the bicycle races, and many of them were bowled over by the cyclists on the track.

Effects of the Bolshevik Revolution

By May, 1917, soldiers at the Voenny-Gorodok and other military centers near Irkutsk were trying to start schools and clubs for themselves. By summer this movement was well under way, organized by the Association in three centers, the 22nd Battery, the 718th Regiment, and the 715th Regiment. Here and there officers were starting clubs for soldiers; there was a large gymnasium in the city, widely patronized by civilians, especially the youngsters, by the soldiers, and by the military staff. The work was very popular; and on one occasion an American secretary heard a Russian priest, while preaching on a revival of the moral and religious life of the city, strongly commend the YMCA and prophesy better days for the city because of it. But, by September, 1917, the Bolshevik agitation began to appear along with anarchistic propaganda in the form of leaflets and speeches to soldiers. Russian officers who had helped the Association became marked men. The Bolsheviks tried to get the Y committees under their control; the schools were discontinued, the library was closed. The workers on the building began to demand more pay and agitators induced the men to refuse to work. Y officials were accused of being bourgeois. The clouds gathered till the revolution broke in December, 1917. Activities then ceased and the secretary and his family escaped from Irkutsk as best they could.

Y Work in Garrison Cities and on the Fronts

When the American Mission to Russia arrived in Petrograd in June, 1917, therefore, the YMCA had already made several practical demonstrations of successful activity among Russian soldiers. After several conferences with Prince Lvov, the former Premier, Kerensky, then Minister of War, Tereshchenko, Minister of Foreign Affairs, and other Russian leaders, it was evident that Russians of all classes would unite in welcoming a widespread activity among soldiers of the Russian Army by representatives of the American YMCA. Messages were cabled to America calling upon the Association to put forth a special effort to assist.

It was decided to undertake the work without delay. To that end all the available YMCA secretaries in Russia were summoned to Petrograd to receive new assignments and instructions. In June and July, 1917, two men were sent to Minsk, the principal base behind the West Front in Russia, two to Moscow, two to Odessa, one to Kazan, one to Irkutsk, and one was assigned to Petrograd. These men had at their disposal nothing but their own personality and goodwill, for the Association had no suitable supplies. Moreover, official endorsements and recommendations had not then been obtained from the Provisional Government. Official permits came in the course of the summer and fall; but by the time they were received they were worthless in many cases, because the authority that issued them was no longer actually functioning. Kerensky became premier July 20, 1917. From the very first his authority was questioned by the soldiers' and workmen's deputies, and by November 6th his government was definitely overthrown. These political and social changes hampered the secretaries severely, while the army that they were supposed to serve was rapidly vanishing as a result of enemy and Bolshevik propaganda. During the early days of 1918 Russia was negotiating a separate peace with Germany. The Brest-Litovsk Treaty was signed in March. This eventually put an end to Y work for the Russian Army. Such is the political background now to be described.

The Khodynka Hut, Moscow

The first Red Triangle Hut was set in operation at the Khodynka Camp, near Moscow, on July 28, 1917, just a day and a half after the building had been turned over to the Association representatives. Thousands of Russian recruits passing through this camp preparatory to their dispatch to the various fronts used the facilities of the YMCA during the months of August and September, 1917. As each regiment went to the front from its encampment, the Y had a special meeting for them, and sent them musical instruments, books and a quantity of writing paper and pencils; sometimes a football or two. The secretary gave them a message of encouragement and friendship from America in his broken Russian, and his appearance was nearly always greeted by cheers from the soldiers who showed their appreciation by tossing him on their shoulders in true Russian style. This "Soldatsky Dom" or Soldier's House, as it was called, went along quietly and successfully until the middle of February when an American Bolshevik broke loose in a tirade against it. Somewhat later the Army melted away and the Soldatsky Dom became a thing of the past.

The Dissolving Army

After the conference for reassignment in July, 1917, the secretaries faced the hard situation courageously and went to their various posts. Out on the field a silent tragedy was enacted; there day by day, these few workers, helpless to stem the current, watched the Russian forces melt away.

Three different workers in succession struggled in Kazan but very little could be accomplished. In October, 1917, a soldiers' club and a tea room were started in Kiev. A new group of soldiers came in and commandeered the center for an unending series of Bolshevik meetings. A second building was secured at Peterchsky Barracks but the whole enterprise, hampered at every point, had to be abandoned in February, 1918, on the approach of the German and Ukrainian Armies. When an attempt to open at Kharkov was made in October, the Bolsheviks were practically in power; and there was no settled authority with which to deal. The secretary managed to promote a few activities till March, 1918; when he left, some Russian helpers tried to continue but without success. On the western front, a fairly extensive service, centering in Minsk, was begun amid great enthusiasm: a Minsk club and a Polish club in the city and five huts near the lines at Salescia, Ponesia, Emovshezma, and Bloc Post. After heartrending delays these centers were opened in December and January; but, of course, the process of disintegration had gone far and deep, and by February, 1918, they were all evacuated. The Russian front had ceased to exist. In the Caucasus a group of six workers, entering Tiflis[11] January 1, 1918, found the only opportunity was in connection with a proposed National Army in process of formation. A club was opened in Yerevan on February 15, 1918, but was closed soon after on the advice of the American Consul. Finally, on April 16th, the Caucasian enterprise was abandoned. Two secretaries remained to carry on a remarkable piece of relief work among the Armenians. Things were no better in the north. Three clubs were started

---

[11] Today Tbilisi, Georgia.

at Dvinsk,[12] but the hut at Pvov was closed by the Bolsheviks almost at once. Two men in the Don region and one man with cavalry regiments on the southern front made little headway. At Odessa, some progress was made. A large building, opened October 6, 1917, operated with a full program in the heart of the soldier community, while a second center—formerly the gayest and most luxurious "cafe chantant" in the city—opened on February 22nd, reached the sailors as well, very effectively. A feeding train operated from March 7 to April 4, 1918, on the northern front serving 10,000 men, including war prisoners and invalids. This ended the activity of the Y with the Russian Army on the fighting fronts and in the garrisons.

The service was not without achievement, for the files of the YMCA are full of messages of heartfelt appreciation from Russian soldiers, but it was a losing game. Some secretaries withdrew from their posts, others were recalled, still others on the earnest appeal of the Acting Senior Secretary stuck it out till the positions were untenable. All in actual touch with the situation knew with certainty that there was only one end possible.

From the Samara Conference to the Period of Allied Intervention

As will be seen from the foregoing account, by February, 1918, work for the Russian Army had broken down for the simple reason that the Army ceased to exist as a fighting unit. The Association had to change its policy to meet a new situation. This was done at a conference at Samara, early in March, 1918. One of the most interesting dramas played on this Russian stage was that of the conflict of interests and ideals on the part of the men who were responsible for the work in Russia. In the first place the great political and military events which were affecting the work of the Association so adversely happened during what might be called an interregnum in administrative authority. A. C. Harte, who had the supervision of the War Prisoners' Aid in Russia as well as in other countries of Europe, was originally responsible for the Russian Army work. He left Russia in the summer of 1917, delegating his authority to an acting Senior Secretary, Jerome Davis, with whom was associated Crawford Wheeler, until his proposed return in October, 1917. He could not return to Russia, however, and his successor, E. T. Colton, who was appointed on December 5, 1917, did not actually arrive in Russia until March, 1918. Thus, during this entire critical period the administration was in the hands of men whose tenure of office was temporary and who did not feel themselves in a position to make decisions of the most vital importance. In the meanwhile the most fundamental issues were clamoring for a settlement.

---

[12] Today Daugavpils, Latvia.

Reactions on Different Temperaments

In the Association group, as in all groups, were men of the most diverse temperaments. When events did not bear out high hopes and expectations and the work collapsed, the reactions of the different types of men were characteristic. Some moved on to the next practical consideration, which for most of the younger men of military age was to get out of Russia and into the Allied Armies as soon as possible. Others felt that the Allied cause might be served better by their remaining in Russia and engaging in non-military welfare work. To others, conceivably, international and humanitarian ideals loomed larger than national considerations of any character whatsoever. On the basis of these temperamental differences and conceptions of moral obligation individuals made decisions and acted. Their actions and the consequences can be traced to these differences of personality, which really lie at the foundation of all action and all history.

Administrative History to the Samara Conference

A conference between Association leaders was held in the Winter Palace, Petrograd, June 27, 1917. It was hoped at the time that the contemplated plan for Russian soldiers would serve as the basis for a permanent piece of Association work, and that societies similar to the *Mayak* would be established throughout Russia. Consequently in July, 1917, Dr. Harte called on the Chief of Staff of the Russian Armies asking permission to start work on a large scale. This request was referred to Mr. Kerensky.

On July 13, 1917, the Soldiers' Deputies granted the YMCA permission to organize a soldiers' club in Moscow. On August 13, 1917, the Military Staff authorized the Association to work in the central cities of Russia but prohibited it from working in the armies near the front. On August 29, 1917, the Military Governor of Moscow, Mr. Verkhovsky,[13] later Minister of War under the Kerensky Government, wrote a public testimonial to the high value of the Association activities in Moscow and asked all authorities to help the Association establish its work on the broadest possible scale. On September 5, 1917, following a personal interview with Kerensky, permission was granted to start the regular Association activities along all the fronts of the Russian Army. On October 12, 1917, the political department of the temporary government issued a document asking that all organizations help the Association and that the railroads grant all requests for shipment of supplies and railroad tickets.

On October 20, 1917, following conferences with the Minister of Justice, Minister of Foreign Affairs, Minister of War, Commander-in-Chief of the Russian Armies and Premier, the Kerensky Cabinet unanimously passed the following resolution:

---

[13] Alexander I. Verkhovsky (1886–1938), a high-ranking Russian army officer, served as minister of war in the Provisional Government from August 30, 1917, to October 21, 1917.

The spreading of the Young Men's Christian Association activities both at the front of our active army and in the rear, as well as in France and Saloniki, is considered desirable and deserving of encouragement in every way. In order to assist the Association to do this, the said Association is hereby granted the following privileges:

I. Transportation of all goods belonging to the Association free of charge and immediately without waiting turn on all the railroads.

II. Selling of railroad tickets to the employees of the Association without delay or hindrance.

III. Sending of soldiers' letters written in the Club and provided with the Association mark, free of charge.

IV. Exempting of all goods coming from abroad for the necessities of the YMCA from custom duties and all other taxes.

At that time Dr. Harte was expected to be in Russia to take up the responsibility for the work. In October and November the new recruits for the Russian work, over 50 in all, arrived in three groups, and were assigned to their posts, but the Bolshevik revolution broke and chaos set in.

Moscow Conference

Early in December the Association men who could be gathered in Moscow held a conference in regard to their course of action. Should Association work still be carried on by Americans who were sent to Russia to keep the Army at the front? Some had decided to return. American and Russian officials urged their remaining, and the following cablegram was set to New York:

A Conference of forty secretaries from the field and in training reveals the fact that there are now few places of contact with the Army and the existing conditions make work of direct military value impossible on Russian fronts. There are no signs of early improvement.

A wire received through the embassy urges the Association to fullest effort, but we question here whether it was sent with knowledge of recent events. Some men are ready to stay so long as work of any kind remains, others recruited in New York on war basis are disposed to seek service elsewhere. The Conference (1) recommends that authority be wired to Russian executive committee to act regarding transfer of such individuals to other Allied fronts or their release; (2) requests advice whether it is justified in spending war money in civil and permanent work; (3) advises that it has constituted following executive committee, including war work secretary, financial secretary, Christy, Story, Halsey, Wheeler; (4) urges that above committee be recognized, made permanent and wired full authorization to deal with Russian war work. Meanwhile action is imperative and committee will go ahead.

By action of this "distinctly revolutionary gathering," as one secretary termed it, the Association decided to continue with its work for the time being until authority could be turned over to persons delegated by the National War Work Council to receive it.

Samara Conference

When the secretaries were all called together for conference at Samara in March, 1918, on the arrival of Mr. Colton, Senior Secretary, there were 73 representatives of the American YMCA in different parts of Russia. About 20 had arrived only recently from America after a long-delayed passage through England, Sweden, Finland and Arctic ports into Central Russia. Many of them wished to leave Russia and return to America to join the Army. Some desired to go direct by sea to France. Some of those who had long been in Russia felt that they could be of more service by staying. The following cable message from Dr. John R. Mott was read in the conference:

> I urge secretaries to remain in Russia. In my recent personal conference with President Wilson he strongly approved of all men remaining who were already in Russia when America entered the war; also other men who were not subject to draft before they left America; for purposes helping in friendly Association work for men of all parties and classes in every possible way, demonstrating unselfish interest of America in Russian people. Other members of our Government consulted by me concur in this advice. The twelve men delayed in England are going forward. I will send more secretaries for extension of work when you request same.

Action of Individual Secretaries

After considerable open debate, every man stated his decision. Eleven men felt that they must leave Russia in order to make themselves available for military service in the United States forces. Six others were compelled to start homeward because of health or other personal reasons. The remaining 56 men stated preference for various types of service with people in Russia.

Those who remained in the YMCA were assigned by the Senior Secretary to various fields of work. Sixteen went to Moscow, of whom seven were to be engaged in relief service among returning Russian prisoners of war, three in carrying on a civilian program among the people of Moscow, and six others in executive and financial capacities. Five men were assigned to Samara, four to Kazan and two to Nizhny Novgorod, cities along the Volga River. One man was sent to Petrograd, and two started for Archangelsk and Murmansk. The two men in Yerevan continued operations and three secretaries from the *Mayak* in Petrograd began a civilian program in Vladivostok. Six sturdy-hearted individuals expressed their determination to share with the Czechoslovak divisions whatever fate might be in store for them. Two others undertook to convoy a trainload of Serbian refugees across Siberia, and one attached himself to a battalion of Serbian soldiers en route to France via the Arctic ports. Three rural specialists set out to investigate possibilities for work among the peasants along the Volga River. The six remaining men entered the American Consular service. Thus the personnel was reassigned on the basis of the new work and a fresh start was made. Of course, the whole situation changed fundamentally a few months later as a result of the military intervention of the Allies.

Civil and Military Work in Samara, Summer of 1918

After the Samara Conference the attention of the Association was devoted primarily to city work, while standing ready to serve any military organizations which might exist or be created. Already the Czechoslovaks were becoming the center of military interest, and new anti-Bolshevik armies among which the Association was destined to cast its lot were about to be organized.

At Samara, the Association took over all sorts of civilian and relief work. Most of the Red Cross workers had left Russia, on advice of the American Ambassador, when the Treaty of Brest-Litovsk was concluded. Red Cross funds, however, were put at the disposal of the Association. Immediately after the Samara Conference early in March, it assumed responsibility for a maternity home. A company of 700 Boy Scouts was also discovered, which had been organized by the boys themselves, without adult leadership, on the basis of some translations of Scout documents. An athletic director took hold of this work and made it very successful. There were some educational lectures and later a conference on the entire lecture program of the Association in Russia. A group of Serbian refugees was discovered and cared for. A feeding point and later a hospital were opened for all refugees near the station and hundreds were fed daily. Groups of Jewish and Polish refugees were helped and a large number of students of both sexes who were quite without support were given employment. There was a school for physical directors and a large and successful playground program.

On the military side there were three Soldiers' Clubs—one on the main street, Dvoryanskaya, centrally located, for the soldiers of the new Russian National Army; one for the Czechoslovaks near the station where these troops were quartered in cars; and one in the artillery barrack where the new recruits for the Russian Army were sent. There were also club-cars, or wagon-huts as they were called—large American box cars remodeled into canteens which traveled up and down the front giving "movies" under a rain of shrapnel. On one occasion three men were wounded as the others sat quietly under their steel helmets and enjoyed the show. Other cars were prepared and sent out along the Trans-Siberian Railway with the Czechoslovaks, where they became an essential part of the Y service.

Nizhny Novgorod

The Association in Nizhny secured fine rooms in the center of the city and conducted classes in gymnastics and English during the evening. Preparations had already been made for other activities and for close cooperation with the rural department in its work from this center, when all plans were interrupted by the exodus from Soviet Russia of all American secretaries.

City Work in Moscow, Summer of 1918

When the Russian armies disbanded, the Moscow soldiers' club was opened by all young men. Work for boys in cooperation with the Boy Scout movement, was carried on in a separate building. The Association also participated with the Student Christian Movement in evangelistic work. An attempt was made to do athletic work with the unstable Red Army, but this was unsuccessful.

Volga Agricultural Exhibition

Aided by the local government who granted the use of a large river boat with fuel and crew, and with the wholehearted support of the American Red Cross and American business firms, Russian Cooperative Societies, and other rural organizations, the Rural Department of the YMCA organized the Volga Agricultural Expedition during the summer of 1918, for the purpose of educating the people in rural work and interests. The equipment included exhibits illustrating improved methods in dairying, stock raising, bee keeping, field crops, horticulture, poultry, principles of cooperation, care of children, care of the home, sanitation, farm machinery and the like. A staff of 31 Russian experts, who understood the peasant problems and needs, aided with films, slides and charts. During the interval from June until about mid-August this expedition visited 44 towns along the Volga River in the heart of Russia, presenting their material before more than 30,000 men and women, a service commended by the clergy through Patriarch Tikhon of Moscow who wrote:

> The YMCA is undertaking the support of a series of movements having for their object the improvement of the moral atmosphere of Russian life; the preaching of God's word; and, abstaining from politics, cooperating with Russian educational and economic improvement societies. Sympathizing

with everything which may be helpful materially or morally, to our Russian people, we hereby confer our blessing upon the organizers of this good work, praying God's aid for its successful accomplishment.

Summary of Civilian Work, 1918

Nothing could have been a more unmistakable witness to the goodwill of the American people toward Russian than this civilian work. As in so much of its work during the war, the Association became the channel through which the humanitarian impulse of America found free expression. Practically all the Association workers had gone to Russia to do war work. Their disappointment was great when this became impossible. The Russian people sadly needed help. The Association forces constituted the only available agency by which America could reach them. Though this work which centered in Samara seemed at the time but an interlude between two great military episodes, it marked the beginning of relations which may prove the most permanent and significant result of the Russian enterprise. Although brought to an end in Soviet Russia, it was continued in the larger cities of Siberia during the next year and is still thriving in Vladivostok and Harbin. Its effect was a profound impression upon thousands of Russians that America was generously and efficiently concerned in promoting the welfare of their people.

Period of Allied Intervention

Military intervention in Russia was determined upon by the Supreme War Council at Versailles in the spring of 1918 as a strategic measure. The idea was to reestablish an eastern front on the Volga River in order to divert the German forces by bringing Russia back into the war and to prevent the Germans from taking the extensive munition works in the industrial cities of that region. Military action in Siberia also seemed necessary for the protection of Allied supplies in Vladivostok and to combat those German and Austro-Hungarian war prisoners who were at large supporting the Bolsheviks, and incidentally endangering our Allies, the Czechoslovaks, en route through Siberia to the western front in France.

North Russia

In European Russia, intervention took the form of an international force, containing some American engineers and infantry, which was sent to North Russia to prevent the German penetration of Finland, to retain control of the Murmansk railway leading to the only open port in Northern Russia, and to prevent Allied stores in Archangelsk and along the Vologda Railroad from falling into the hands of the Germans. Support was also given to the North Russian Government, and Americans shared with British troops in the severe fighting with Bolsheviks. This brigading of Americans with British troops and their operations under British command against Bolshevik forces, without a formal declaration of war on our part, caused a great deal of criticism and misunderstanding in this country, partly because the men were forced to undergo extreme hardships in an Arctic climate without sufficient food and protection, and partly because many persons were not in sympathy with what were supposed to be British aims in North Russia. The expedition was criticized most severely by those Americans that took part in it. But, though ill-fated, it was an integral part of the Allied policy of the time, and, with the Siberian expedition, attempted to check the Allied loss caused by Russia's peace with Germany in March, 1918. The American Government defined its attitude August 4, 1918:

> Military action is admissible in Russia only to render help and protection to the Czechoslovaks against armed Austrian and German prisoners who are attacking them and to steady any effort at self-government or self-defense in which Russians themselves may be willing to accept assistance—the only present object for which American troops will be employed will be to guard military stores which may subsequently be needed by Russian forces and to render such aid as may be acceptable to the Russians in the organization of their self-defense.
>
> The Japanese and American Governments agreed to send a joint military expedition of a few thousand troops each, "with the purpose of cooperating as a single force in the occupation of Vladivostok and in safe-guarding, insofar as it may, the country to the rear of the westward moving Czechoslovaks." There shall be no "interference with the political sovereignty of Russia," no "intervention in internal affairs 'not even in the local affairs of the limited areas which our military force may be obligated to occupy,'" the single object being "to render such aid as shall be acceptable to the Russian people themselves to gain control of their own affairs, their own territory, their own destiny."

To aid in this undertaking, the United States Government proposed to send a commission of merchants, agricultural experts, labor advisers, representatives of the Red Cross and of the YMCA, to engage in humanitarian, educational, and economic work for the rehabilitation of Russia.

Effects of Intervention

A necessary consequence of this intervention was the withdrawal of the American Embassy and all official representatives of the United States from Soviet Russia or areas controlled by Soviet Government. It became unsafe for Americans to remain in territory where they could receive no protection from their own Government. Activities of any sort were out of the question. Under advice or orders from the Embassy, practically all the secretaries withdrew from Russia. At Novgorod they were arrested at the instance of a German commandant, but were soon released and returned to Moscow whence they made their way out of the country through Finland or the Archangelsk front. There were left just the secretaries with the Czechoslovaks and a few who had been working in Siberia, out of the Soviet territory.

The entire civilian and relief program initiated by the Samara Conference in March was thus perforce abandoned in October. When the Allied forces made their entry into the country, however, there appeared for the first time a possibility of war work on a large scale. With this political and military situation as a background, the story may now be told of the two largest phases of the Y work in Russia.

At Archangelsk and Murmansk

During the winter and spring of 1918, the YMCA was represented at the two Arctic ports of Archangelsk and Murmansk by one or more secretaries. At Murmansk preparations were started for what later became a very important field. YMCA efforts on behalf of the Allied naval units as well as in the relief of Russian refugees, were recognized in several reports made by Allied officials to their Governments.

The two Red Triangle workers stationed at Archangelsk during the spring of 1918 to receive a cargo of supplies then expected from England, met the advance guard of the Allied troops upon their arrival at Archangelsk on August 3rd. Within a few days after the Bolsheviks had left the city, the two buildings which had been their headquarters were turned into centers for YMCA activities. The Y had only this one service point established in the Archangelsk area, however, when American troops to the number of 5,000 landed in the fall; and it was not until the arrival of a party of 25 American workers from Central Russia on October 1st, that real activities for the American and Allied forces were undertaken. These new arrivals were distributed at the base and front points where American troops were stationed, and by early November ten huts were in operation. More secretaries arrived from England during December, and during January, 1919, service in both Murmansk and Archangelsk reached the maximum, maintained, with occasional changes in the location and number of huts, until the Allied forces departed in the summer of 1919. Eight railroad cars were fitted up as portable Y's for canteen and library service along the railroad line towards Vologda. An average of 24 huts was operated by the Association in the Archangelsk area, all but eight of these being located upon the various fronts. Along the Murmansk railroad, six supply cars were kept busy serving the soldiers guarding the lines of communication, and, at four or five points, old buildings were converted into huts to serve garrisons of Allied soldiers. The personnel included nearly a hundred American, Canadian, and British secretaries, besides Russian assistants.

An extensive program of activities was carried on for the American soldiers in Arctic Russia, although the secretaries were hampered in their efforts by the lack of supplies and equipment. Nevertheless, cinema machines were operated in a circuit of huts along the five hundred mile line of communications around the fronts and American films were shown on an average of three nights a week, even at the points most distantly located from Headquarters.

Secretarial Experiences

Four American Y men were captured while carrying on their work at the front among the Allied troops. Four others were decorated—one with the French Croix de Guerre and three with the Cross of St. George of the Russian Army. Two of the captured secretaries were released from their imprisonment in Moscow, together with six American soldiers who had suffered a similar fate, through the efforts of the YMCA representative at Copenhagen, who went into Soviet Russia to secure their release.

When the American troops were mobilized at an embarkation camp near Archangelsk preparatory to their departure for France, the Y established a large hut in the middle of the camp. Here a canteen was operated, cinema shows and concerts given, a baseball league organized and equipped, and meals served to transient officers and many incoming and departing units of troops. On each transport went a Red Triangle secretary with a moderate supply of candies, cigarettes, and the ingredients for cocoa, all of which were supplied to the American soldiers free of charge.

In June, 1919, the Allied YMCA in North Russia found itself faced with the problems of readjustment due to the withdrawal of the majority of the American forces from that section. This withdrawal left the North Russian Army predominantly British and Russian. The YMCA was, however, predominantly American. Obviously the only course was to relieve the American secretaries as soon as sailings could be arranged and British replacements secured. While the majority of American secretaries were relieved in July, a small group of Americans remained to continue work for the Russian troops and to salvage supplies.

Withdrawal of Americans

About August 15th, instructions came from the American Embassy for all Americans to withdraw from this sector. This meant that the Association work, so far as the Americans were concerned, must be closed at once. All secretaries with the exception of an auditor left North Russia by September 2, 1919. This ended the American YMCA's work in North Russia.

Relationships

There was in North Russia some difficulty in relationships with the British, reflecting in a sense the confusion that seemed inherent in this rather ill-fated enterprise. The details are of no particular interest now but there was at first considerable misunderstanding as to whether the American or the British Y was primarily responsible. The difficulty was solved by an arrangement which made the American, Crawford Wheeler, Senior Secretary of the work and the American Y, furnished the operating capital for canteen service. There were about 30 British secretaries; and the supplies were secured almost entirely from the British YMCA, the British Quartermaster, and the British Army and Navy Canteen Board, since no American supplies arrived till the spring of 1919. A British secretary took charge in the Murmansk area, under Mr. Wheeler's direction, in order to facilitate dealings with the British military authorities. These difficulties and misunderstandings did not prevent cordial personal cooperation; and in spite of the many elements of friction in the whole situation, an excellent piece of cooperative service was achieved. By agreement the British Y assumed entire responsibility in June, 1919.

Railroad and River Fronts South of Archangelsk

The Archangelsk expedition, in which there were some 5,000 American troops, mostly of the 339th Infantry, shares with the Siberian expedition the reputation of being the most romantic, as well as the most ill-fated, in which American troops were engaged. In the popular mind, the expeditions are easily confused. There was ice and snow in both places. But, strictly speaking, our troops in Siberia were operating under winter conditions, not differing greatly from those of Northern Minnesota or Saskatchewan. In fact, they were not operating at all in the military sense, whereas our troops in Northern Russia were actually fighting for the greater part of the winter in the North Frigid Zone and well within the Arctic Circle. They suffered from real hardships, intense cold, insufficient food, disease, and a treacherous guerrilla warfare. A few first-hand descriptions of the activity of Y men under these conditions follow.

Christmas time in such a country and under such conditions is apt to make anyone think rather longingly of home. At that time especially it was the Y man's duty to make things as pleasant as possible. Here is the Christmas story of one worker who, incidentally, received the Croix de Guerre for his activity among French troops on the railroad front south of Archangelsk:

> I left for the front at 7:30 a.m., going first as far as verst[14] 448 (the Russian milestones), where I stopped for two hours, till the next train. There I found ten

---

[14] One verst equals approximately .66 miles.

American signal men as blue as a Wisconsin sky. I had breakfast with them, and left them three dozen candles, candy and cigarettes. They responded well. Then I went to the new barracks. There were 50 King's Liverpools. Poor boys!—for they are scarcely more. They had just done six days at the front and had expected to be at their company banquet, and the movie at No. 445. Then, too, their breakfast ration was short; some getting half, some more, and their special Christmas ration had failed to come. Well, I had candy, candles, and cigarettes, and also called them together for a little service. By the time I had finished the Second Chapter of Luke, some were sniffing, and before I got through a short prayer, about half of the poor fellows were sobbing, I felt a bit that way myself!

In describing the work of this secretary, another Y man wrote:

He carries about 60 pounds of stuff along in knapsacks, and distributes from dugout to dugout and trench to trench around the entire front. Sometimes it's cigarettes, sometimes confectionery, of which we have precious little, sometimes it is sweet crackers or gum. Then once a week he holds a brief service in each of the dugouts as he visits the men; and old Major Moody, the Scotch evangelist, goes the rounds with him occasionally to make a most effective little address. I heard one a few days ago. Here in a clearing, dotted with woodpiles, which have been broken and twisted into the weirdest heaps and lines by breaking shells, are a few log houses which serve as base front headquarters for the men. As we finished our rounds that afternoon, the Captain called all the men who were not needed at the front line into one of these houses for a talk. Back they plodded through the snow, weighed down with rifles, cartridge belts and steel helmets. It was an American company. As the Major told some of his touching stories in his rich Scotch brogue, commenting on them briefly by way of a lesson sermon, tears ran unchecked down the cheeks of many of these rough Michigan boys.

Emergency Service

The Allied YMCA was called upon by the General Headquarters Staff of the North Russia Expeditionary Force to render emergency service to a column of troops being moved overland from the Murmansk peninsula to the Archangelsk military area. The distance was 250 miles through forests and snow in twenty below-zero weather. The points at which canteens and rest stations were to be erected were in Nuchka, at a point halfway between Onega and Sorokoe; Onega, where three days' rest enabled the Y to furnish cinema and other entertainment; Chekueva, half way to Obozorshaya, and Chinova, half way between the two latter points. Cocoa and biscuits were to be the chief items furnished in the canteens at all points, but in addition, groceries and cigarettes were provided so that purchases could be made. The other items were given free of charge in all cases. Of this service, one Tommy said:

> Well, we have had a good slice of luck in a way which we never expected. Three YMCA fellows have come here (200 miles from their depot) and set up a fine YM for us with all sorts of comforts, and are going back when we have moved off again. That is jolly fine, don't you think so? It is, I can assure you, far more than any of us expected and it is fully appreciated by us all.

Another said:

> We found a fine American YMCA at this place. The Yankee secretaries gave us a most hearty welcome and led us at once to a counter where cocoa and biscuits were served and they would not let us pay for it. It was fine of them.

The Vaga River Column

Work was started on the river front early in the fall of 1918, serving the so-called Vaga River column, a mixed force of Americans and Canadians—about 2,000 in number—which formed the line furthest South. Huts were opened in various centers, those at Shenkurst and Ust Padenga being nearest the front.

Shenkurst was inhabited by the better class of Russian people and many refugees from Soviet Russia. There were good schools and flourishing cooperative societies here and the inhabitants were very glad to have Allied troops with them, although skeptical of their ability to hold the town against the Bolsheviks. Their skepticism later was justified. The Y was very popular in Shenkurst and performed all kinds of service. It ran a laundry, supplied hospitals, gave Christmas parties for the children, helped to reopen schools, performed regular Y functions, and acted as Army chaplain.

Several secretaries mention the cordial relations of the Y with various classes of society in Shenkurst and especially the very characteristic episode of the kindness of a certain aged abbess to the Y representatives and to the troops. It is a typical example of the Russian character. One secretary writes as follows:

> In the center of the town stands a beautiful convent. On our arrival the abbess sent a message to say that a Russian bath would be ready for us on the following day and she gave instructions to send the boat for our luggage. We called by appointment to see the old lady, presenting a letter from the patriarch. The abbess, who had been at the monastery for 56 years and was still very active in mind and body, was interested to know which of us undertook the religious side of the work and why we did not wear black robes and long hair. She was

a pleasing old soul, full of vitality in spite of her great age. There were three hundred nuns in the convent. They held services in the crypt, fearing that the Bolsheviks would come and loot the costly Icons in the church. The abbess and those living in the convent did their utmost to make the work of the military officers in the place simpler by rendering all kinds of small services. Nothing seemed to be too much trouble for them in the interests of the troops at Shenkurst. On Christmas Day, for instance, she placed at our disposal one of the churches, providing seating accommodations and an organ, crowning her efforts on our behalf by attending herself with a number of nuns.

Conditions during the Retreat

There were several Y huts in Shenkurst, and at Ust Padenga there was a very fine, large hut with a huge fireplace. It was near the front line, however, and in constant danger. In January, 1919, it had to be evacuated as a result of a Bolshevik advance which threw the Vaga column back on Shenkurst, which was also evacuated, and on Kitza. The Y reached its maximum of service during this retreat and evacuation, providing hot drinks for the exhausted soldiers and civilians, giving aid to the wounded and burying the dead. One of the British Y men was decorated for his valor.

This retreat lasted for several days, as the men in an exhausted condition fell back on Kitza. A Y secretary in charge of a convoy of 90 sleds on the way to Shenkurst, contrary to orders, established a feeding station at Kitza. As the towns were evacuated or captured they were burned and thousands of refugees beat a retreat in the snow. The rear guard action was very severe.

One of the most touching tributes to American activity in this entire unfortunate venture in North Russia was an editorial in a Russian newspaper, "The Northern Morning," on the occasion of Memorial Day, 1919. Even in its rather quaint translation it expresses perhaps better than anything else the characteristic reactions of the "Russian Soul" and its essentially poetic trend. After referring to the origin of Memorial Day, the writer continued:

This year our American friends have to pass this day far from their country in our cold Northland, among the graves of the brave heroes who gave their lives for the humanitarian cause of liberation—graves that are henceforth sacred and dear to Russians as well as to Americans. Honor to the fallen! Blessing and eternal rest to these protectors of humanity who gave their lives for the achievement of justice and right. You are dead, but still live, because you defeated darkness and brought light to the living. Sleep quietly, sons of liberty and light. You won from the world never-fading honor and eternal glory. May the cold tundra of Northern Russia, which took you in its arms, not be too heavy for you. With you are your friends; with you are those who will never forget your sacrifice; with you is Russia, long-suffering and martyred Russia, with whom you formed an alliance through your blood. Sleep quietly, fighting eagles!

In Siberia

There were several phases of Y activity in Siberia, one concerning work with American and Allied troops, another with Russian civilian and army work, and still another with the romantic events connected with the movements of the Czechoslovak forces, eastward across Siberia, back to the Ural front, and eventually eastward again to their final evacuation from Vladivostok. Geographical considerations play a large part in the story of this work and the map should constantly be consulted in following it back and forth over the four thousand miles of Siberian steppes between the Urals and the Pacific.

With American and Allied Troops

When the first American troops arrived in Vladivostok in the autumn of 1918, there were altogether less than a dozen YMCA secretaries in Eastern Siberia; and all of them were over-burdened with work for Czech and Russian forces at the front, or guarding lines of communication. The American troops arrived unexpectedly, without Red Triangle workers or welfare equipment, having come from the Philippine Islands as well as from the United States. Not only Americans, but British, French, Japanese, Serbian, Chinese, and Polish contingents claimed the right to use the several small huts maintained for the Czechs in Vladivostok.

The Y did everything in its power to facilitate the establishment of an adequate program of service to the American forces. American secretaries were recruited from among the missionaries and businessmen of China and Japan on short-time contracts. Urgent cables were sent to the Headquarters in New York, asking for large staff reinforcements, supplies, and equipment. Meanwhile, representatives were sent all over the Far East to gather supplies and equipment and rush them to Vladivostok. The Association opened a biscuit factory, a sausage factory, and absorbed the product of two chocolate and candy factories, practically all there was in Eastern Siberia. In February, 1919, there were five Association huts running full blast for the AEF[15] men near Vladivostok. Huts were also in operation at Roskalnye, the Chuchan mines, Spaskoe, Harbin and Khabarovsk.

Films were difficult to obtain. Shipments from the United States were long coming on account of transport difficulties; Major General Graves, commanding the AEF, loaned the Y 100 reels of films from the Signal Corps supply. The Association had

---

[15] American Expeditionary Forces.

another hundred, and cooperation with representatives of the Committee on Public Information[16] secured the use of still further films. Lectures illustrated by stereopticon slides were given at many points. The secretaries who had been in European Russia through the revolution and had crossed Siberia with the refugees and Czech troops made splendid lecturers. In the words of one of the doughboys "they had some stories to tell." At Vladivostok and Harbin, the American YMCA fitted up athletic fields and playgrounds. Athletics were promoted and the necessary supplies furnished.

Difficulties in Obtaining Supplies

Shortage of equipment and supplies hampered this service very seriously. Ill-fortune kept on the heels of Y shipments from America. The first two shipments got as far as Yokohama, Japan, in November, 1918, where they remained until April, 1919, because of the absence of shipping facilities for the last short lap of the journey. The next shipment, $80,000 worth of athletic goods, piled up on a reef. Another load of 1,000 cases of Y goods was jettisoned in order to float a grounded vessel. Until, through General Graves' good offices, space was secured on transports the Association could not get necessary materials through from America.

To conduct the canteen for the AEF, it was, therefore, necessary to purchase supplies in the open market of the Far East. All canteen supplies were sold to soldiers and sailors at cost, though the expense involved in trans-Pacific freight or shipment from Far Eastern ports made the prices somewhat higher than in the United States. As compared, however, with the prices of mercantile and other establishments in Siberia, a country already suffering a famine of manufactured products of all kinds, the Association scale of charges was low. In addition to the foregoing, the Association saved the American soldiers in Siberia thousands of dollars by conducting an exchange, without profit, at a time when there were no banks in operation and when small change was very difficult to secure. The exchange operations with all of the Allied troops in the winter of 1918 and 1919 involved some fifteen or sixteen currencies and a total sum of almost $100,000 per month.

In June, 1919, the 102 American secretaries in Siberia were distributed as follows: Seventeen among the American Expeditionary Forces, fifteen in the Czech Army, twenty for Russian work, both army and civilian, ten to the International Hut and other Allied units, seven to the executive bureau, twelve to the lecture bureau (including eight cinema experts), eight to finance, four to supply, two to the railway and seven to the rural departments. The work among the American Expeditionary Forces was carried on in ten separate huts and fourteen isolated posts as extension service from hut centers. In the Czech Army fifteen clubs and eighteen canteen cars

---

[16] US government agency organized to promote public support for the war effort, in operation from 1917 to 1919.

were maintained along the line of 1,800 miles of railroad guarded by the Czech troops. Huts or canteen cars were also maintained for the Italians, the Romanians, the French, the British, the Poles, the Serbian units, and the Chinese troops.

Association Activities

During the rest of the year, 1919, every effort was made to increase the service of the Association for the American troops in Siberia with an average personnel of 90 secretaries. Not only were huts maintained in all the centers where any considerable detachment of American soldiers were established, but traveling "movie" cars and canteen cars served the isolated men, with instructions to stop wherever there were even five or six men. In the early fall of 1919 the New York office sent out experienced entertainment units who had made good with the AEF in France, besides other units which went out from Japan. Experienced and tried men went out as lecturers and as religious work leaders, together with a male quartet, practically all of whom were also specialists in the leading of mass singing. The Association shipped monthly from the New York office 100,000 feet of film, 60,000 pounds of chocolate and 1,000,000 cigarettes, the last two items for free distribution to the American troops alone. A special corps of workers kept in circulation and repair the 600,000 feet of film that went out in monthly installments and took many thousands of feet of local scenes for use among the troops.

Christmas, 1919, a year and more after the Armistice, still found the AEF in Siberia and the Y still standing by, providing every man with a Christmas present and a little Christmas cheer. The expedition was not finally withdrawn until the next spring (1920). The Y stayed in Siberia until the end of 1920 and did its largest work in connection with the evacuation of the American troops, the Czechoslovaks, and the Allies.

Work with Russian Civilians in the Far East

In accordance with the decisions of the Samara conference, those secretaries who were interested primarily in constructive work in Russia began to look for fields of activity in various Russian and Siberian cities. After September, 1918, this work was necessarily confined to the non-Bolshevik Russia.

In the spring of 1918, there were eight men in Vladivostok engaged in city work, in addition to service for American marines in cooperation with officers and chaplains. These men were engaged in such specialties as refugee relief, education, and boys' work. In Harbin there was also instituted both railroad and Russian community work. This effort included physical education in several of the largest Russian schools, very successfully handled by Russian secretaries. There was also a city gymnasium and educational movies. Relations with the Church were cordial and one priest cooperated actively. The railroad work was conducted primarily for the American Engineers, who were located in Harbin and along the Chinese Eastern Railway and for their Russian employees, and consisted of a very popular club at the Engineers' barrack near the station.

In Khabarovsk there was both soldier and civilian work after May, 1919, when civilian work which was called the *Mayak*, as it had been years earlier in Petrograd, was opened. There was a successful athletic program and other typical city features and the work made a good impression on the people of the city, which is one of the most enterprising in the Far East.

Central Siberia

During the fall of 1918 and all through 1919 both army and civilian work was carried on in Irkutsk. The civilian work included, besides regular city work, several large and successful playgrounds and boy scout activities. The total attendance at all activities operated by the Association for the month of November, 1919, was 16,170. The work had the cooperation and sympathy of the best elements in the population of Irkutsk and enthusiastic testimonials were received from Russian welfare societies.

A secretary who had done successful civilian work in Samara during the summer of 1918, and later had operated several soldiers' clubs in Ekaterinburg, went to Tomsk in March, 1919, and carried on successful civilian work for the rest of the year. Seven playgrounds were in operation throughout the summer, carried on with the aid of twenty Russian assistants, and a school for 300 refugee children. During the fall, up to the evacuation of Tomsk by anti-Bolshevik forces, a buffet was operated at cost prices for the daily benefit of a thousand students in the University. This was a great saving to students not only in money but in time. A language school was offered on lines not given by the University but necessary for the students in taking certain courses. This work not only had the hearty endorsement of the student body and the leading members of the Faculty, but the Minister of Education from Omsk personally commended it upon his visit to the University in October, 1919.

In Novo-Nikolaevsk,[17] three playgrounds were operated during the summer of 1919 for the children of the community, and for the railway employees. Over 900 people were enrolled in educational classes. At the invitation of the garrison general, regular moving picture shows were given to the military hospitals and the soldiers in the city, and supplies of cigarettes and chocolate were distributed weekly to the invalids. The work in Novo-Nikolaevsk was one of the finest examples of the community type of work that has been done by the YMCA. The military, church, educational, and city authorities all gave splendid support, and courteously expressed

---

[17] Today Novosibirsk, Russia.

their thanks in letters when the work had to be closed as a result of the Bolshevik advance of the fall of 1919.

There was city work in Omsk, but in the spring of 1919 the Y forces retired to Irkutsk as headquarters, and soon after the military situation made Y work in Western Siberia impossible.

Rural Work

The retreat of the Kolchak Army in the summer and fall of 1919 forced the closing of work for Russian civilians in a number of cities. By December, 1919, these had been reduced to Irkutsk, Harbin, and Vladivostok. Permission had been granted for the YMCA to develop its work for the rural communities. The plan presented, modeled on rural work carried on in America by the YMCA, met with the whole-hearted approval of the Zemstvos, Cooperatives, and other conservative rural leaders. Unfortunately conditions did not permit the long continuation of this work.

In the city work emphasis had been placed on the development of physical, educational, and social activities. In every way possible the Y tried to aid local Russian institutions. The development of the playgrounds in several centers mentioned materially influenced the children and was greatly appreciated by the parents. Moving pictures were used primarily as an educational feature. English classes, athletics, such as volley ball and basket ball, summer camps for boys, cooperation with scouts, adoption and development of the Christian Citizenship Training Program for Russians, school for illiterate children, movies in schools and school children brought in as a body to the Y for special lectures on health and other subjects, teacher training classes, financial campaigns among Russians conducted by Russian YMCA secretaries to secure money to help refugees, training class for workers with girls and boys, were a few of the Y activities for civilians. This civilian work had the support of the Orthodox Church, and there is undoubtedly a great future for it in Russia. The Russians are essentially a sociable people who have given expression to their social interest in such institutions as the Narodny Dom (People's House) and the social (including the athletic and educational) features of Y work make a great appeal to them. The religious approach is more difficult, as in religion the Russians incline more to mystical than to practical, applied Christianity. But it can safely be assumed that the future will see a great development in social and welfare work in Russia. There is certainly great need for it in connection with the tremendous enterprise of Russian reconstruction.

Russian Army Work: The Omsk Government

Before the period of Allied intervention in Russia and during the beginnings of the civilian work just described, local Soviets were in control in practically all of the cities of Siberia. This control was broken during the spring and summer of 1918 by the Czechoslovaks. In their effort to get out of Siberia by way of Vladivostok to fight on the French front, they were detained by the Soviets, came into conflict with them and finished by taking all the important towns on the railway. Opportunity to establish themselves was thus given to other elements in Russian society. On July 4, 1918, the Provisional Siberian Duma, meeting at Tomsk, put the affairs of Siberia into the hands of a government, sometimes called the Autonomous Siberian Government. Later, this government joined a group from Ufa, formerly connected with the Constituent Assembly in Russia that had been broken up by the Bolsheviks in January, 1919. This "All-Russian Government" under the head of Mr. Akvsentiev, could not enforce law and order, and after the Armistice and the voluntary withdrawal of the Czechoslovaks from the Ural front, the ministry put the government into the hands of Admiral Kolchak,[18] November 18, 1918.

The obvious task of the new government was to raise an army that could take the place of the Czechoslovak forces. Heroic efforts were made and with the help of British equipment material, several thousand men were put in the field within a few months. The Y was requested by the Omsk government to furnish this new Siberian army its accustomed service for the sustaining and upbuilding of military morale.

Consul General Harris, the American representative in Omsk, notified Washington of this important request in these words:

> The Foreign Department of the Russian Government at Omsk, on February first, appealed officially to the YMCA organization to extend its operations to the new Russian Army. This was done after the Government had satisfied itself that the YMCA carried on no political propaganda. The Government further requested that the YMCA refrain from the employment of Russian Jews in connection with work in Russia. It desires that all the work in connection with the Russian Army be conducted exclusively by American secretaries. The Government is arranging for the appointment of an officer from the General Staff to act in connection with YMCA in working out the details of a program and to assist in all matters of practical cooperation. The Government has under favorable consideration special legislation which will continue the privileges of free transportation and will assist in all matters of practical cooperation, and free customs which was granted YMCA by former Kerensky government. It appears, however, that these privileges have been enjoyed by them in Siberia until present time, but Government wishes to confirm it by special act. The Cossacks have also made an appeal to YMCA to extend operation to their soldiers and people in the Orenburg and

---

[18] Alexander V. Kolchak (1874–1920) served as an admiral in the Imperial Russian Navy and led an anti-Bolshevik government based in Omsk from 1918–20.

Semipalatinsk districts. They are offering every possible facility in connection with the work.

Those in charge of YMCA work here are planning extensions of their activity to the Siberian Army, Czechs, Romanians, Serbians and Poles on a large scale. A request has been made for two hundred secretaries. I do not consider the demand excessive. I believe in doing the work well, and the organization thus got together in Siberia can be moved into European Russia when the proper time comes. I recommend the plan and hope it will be carried out.

Effect of President Wilson's Conference Proposal

Before this request could be definitely acted upon by Y authorities in Vladivostok, President Wilson made his proposal of a conference of all Russian factions at Princes' Island. This altered the attitude of the Omsk Government to Americans for a time at least, and made Russians far less cordial to American participation in their affairs. The Acting Foreign Minister was still favorable, and Y secretaries on the front looked forward to work with the new Russian Army.

Suddenly the whole situation changed during the latter half of March, and the Y was requested by the Russian General Staff to cease work on the front, on the ground that the Government was afraid to risk any outside influence there during the extremely critical period. The "outside influence" feared was that of Russian Jewish interpreters in the employ of the Y who were supposed to be engaged in Bolshevik propaganda. This seems to be a moot point. Y officials disclaimed having any such persons in their employ at that time, and the whole affair may have been a misunderstanding. The Allied General Staff reported, however, to American military officials in Omsk at the time, that a car bearing the inscription "American Mission" (by which title the Y was known there) was circulating at the front, distributing Bolshevik propaganda to the Siberian Army and arms to the enemy. This rumor or fact, whichever it might have been, coupled with the confusion of the Red Triangle (when double) with the Hebrew six-pointed star, and other misapprehensions too ludicrous to mention, were too much for the nervous officials of the Omsk Government, who were staking all on the army. The misunderstanding might have been avoided had Y officials in Vladivostok really appreciated the situation in Omsk, especially the effect of certain rulings in regard to canteen service, which affected the Russian officer class adversely, or had the Omsk representatives been seasoned diplomats. It is not clear from the records available just what secret influence, if any, was behind the whole matter. As a result of the request of the Omsk Government, the Y recalled the seven secretaries west of Omsk and shortly removed its headquarters to Irkutsk. That town subsequently became the center of opposition to the Omsk Government and was the place where Kolchak was put to death, February 7, 1920, by the Social Revolutionary Government that held sway there at the time. The whole story of this period is not yet clear but apparently Kolchak and those he represented were caught between the Monarchists and the Social Revolutionists.

With the Czechoslovak Forces

After the Russian revolution, 1917, the former Czechoslovak war prisoners in South Russia were permitted by the Russian authorities to recruit and organize an army from the Czech prisoners of war. By July, 1917, three regiments of infantry had been formed, and these regiments took an active part in the "Kerensky" offensive of that month. The Czechs, unaided, and lacking much in the way of equipment, captured six of the enemy lines, and pressed on to within striking distance of Lvov. Russian and even German officers who witnessed their charge at Zborov testify that they never saw its like for rapidity and ferocity. They were also able to render heroic service in covering the retreat upon Tarnopol,[19] and it is due to their efforts that much material and many men were saved from the enemy. During this period of fighting the Czechs won a great name for themselves.

This acted as a great stimulus to recruiting, and within two months an entire army corps had been formed, and was ready for further fighting. But the Czechs were condemned to long months of waiting—watchful and very nervous waiting. All about them were signs of disorganization and anarchy. Each week that passed brought news of further internal strife. It was a situation full of dangers to the discipline and morale of the men. Yet the Czechoslovak Army maintained its discipline and its morale, and came through the winter of 1917 the only organized and disciplined fighting force in Russia. In the internal dissensions within Russia the Czechs took absolutely no part. They were organized to fight against the Central Powers until the freedom of Bohemia was won, and nothing could swerve them from that course. They would have preferred to fight in Russia on the side of Russia and they lingered in Russia until they saw that nothing could be looked for there in the way of a strong army. Then they decided to go where they could be of some use.

The only way out of Russia that was open to them was that across Siberia. That meant the transportation of an entire army corps some 6,000 miles to Vladivostok, thence by boat to France. Most people would have been staggered by the magnitude of the task, but not the Czechs. They secured the support of the French Government, had themselves recognized as a part of the independent Czechoslovak Army in France, secured some 60 troop trains and set out on their way. It was with these intrepid Bohemian nationalists that the Y had already cast its fortunes.

---

[19] Today Ternopil, Ukraine.

Division of the Czechoslovak Forces

The story has two parts. One concerns the extreme western part of Siberia, where the Czechoslovak National Council and Military Staff were located; the other, the extreme eastern part of Siberia, at Vladivostok, where some 15,000 of the 67,000 Czechoslovaks had arrived in May, 1918, and were awaiting transportation to France.[20]

Trouble between the Czechs and the Bolsheviks arose at Chelyabinsk and along the line in May, 1918. Aided by Austrian and German prisoners, the Bolsheviks held up the Czechoslovaks at various points and closed the tunnels south of Lake Baikal, thus cutting communications between the two parts of the force. News of this reached the Czechs at Vladivostok, who proceeded to occupy the city and sent forces to the aide of their comrades. In September, the tunnels at Lake Baikal were seized, and the entire force drew gradually eastward. Through all this, Association workers were constantly with both sections, accompanying them back and forth between Vladivostok and the Ural front.

The Y Joins the Czechs

Perhaps the best approach to this intricate but romantic story is the personal account of a Y secretary who was in charge of the work for the Czechs from the start. The following are excerpts:

> I arrived at Kiev in the midst of the Bolshevik revolution, and disorders that followed did much to delay the opening of our work with the Czechs and to hamper it after it was going. Probably the world has seen few scenes of more riotous disorder than those accompanying the return of the Russian "comrades" from the front in the last months of 1917. I was obliged to ride on the roofs of cars, or perched out on the step in order to make the journey from Kiev to the front. But it was inspiring to find the little band of Czechoslovaks calmly proceeding with the organization of their revolutionary army while Russia was going to pieces around them.
>
> Finally, near the end of December, our equipment arrived, consisting of a number of portable buildings and the usual supplies for equipping the same Y hut features. We opened the first hut on Christmas Eve Old Style, January 6th New Style, at the Staff Headquarters of the First Division at Polonnoe, 270 versts west of Kiev and about 100 versts back of the actual front. The men were billeted around the little Ukrainian villages, sleeping on the dirt floor,

---

[20] [Footnote in original text] The political headquarters were at Ekaterinburg and the military staff was located at Chelyabinsk.

and they often had no candles in the evening, and nowhere to go except out in the muddy street, so that they welcomed our hut with great enthusiasm, and crowded it every day and every evening to its utmost capacity.

A few days later, Mr. Atherton, who was with me, opened up a larger plant at the Second Regiment, and a week or so after I opened another small hut at the Third Regiment, occupying an old thatched covered cottage. In addition, we were able to supply every regiment of the army with a good-sized library of Russian books, for use in the regimental and company libraries that they had already founded. We also cooperated with the men in the arrangement of a number of theatrical performances, concerts and dances, generally using an old barn for the purpose. The opportunities for service there with the men quartered throughout the villages were tremendous, and we were just beginning to really get hold of the situation when the order came to move. Our huts had been in operation just three weeks, but there was nothing to do but to pack up our equipment, and move along. The faithful Czechs not only took our property with them, but guarded it carefully through all vicissitudes of their journey during the next few months, and a good part of it is now set up and in daily operation on the plains of Siberia, three thousand versts away from our original location.

Each Y man fitted out a car for himself, and as the Czech troop trains came along the cars were attached and the men started on their way to Vladivostok, with a good supply of reading matter, games, and athletic equipment to keep the men occupied at the stops. Two men reached Vladivostok, others were detained in the region of Chelyabinsk, and still others in Central Siberia.

Chelyabinsk

At this point (May, 1918) actual hostilities broke out between the Czechs and the Bolsheviks. It soon became plain that the lines were blocked east and west, so the Y opened on June 9th a hut at the railroad station in Chelyabinsk. There were some 8,000 men in this locality. A first-rate program was inaugurated; and though there was no communication with the outside world, the Y was able to secure supplies locally. A bakery and a sausage factory were established so the men could secure the kind of rolls and sausage to which they were accustomed. Butter and cheese were plentiful. Every week a refrigerator car was dispatched to one or another of the fronts with cold drinks, sausage, cheese, and butter. As the Czech forces proceeded with the clearing of the Urals, the fronts developed at a distance from Chelyabinsk and besides its welfare work, the efforts of the Y, in the absence of any Red Cross organization, were devoted to the wounded.

Ekaterinburg

A little later, an extensive service was opened in Ekaterinburg, still within the zone of the Czechoslovaks, where all privileges were accorded the YMCA. At this point there were several thousand Russians in addition to the Czechs. Three clubs were opened in the city and one outside for the outposts, a soldiers' store was established at the station, and work was carried on in two hospitals and an invalid home. On some days 10,000 men were served. In the Czech Club there was an orchestra and a Bohemian coffee room managed by six women who spoke the Czech language. The people of the city helped to furnish the club rooms. The little store sometimes handled 500 pounds of bread and 400 pounds of sausage in a single day. In the Russian Club there was a lecture, concert, vaudeville, or moving picture show every night. A bureau for returning Russian prisoners completed a round of activities possibly the most extensive carried on in the course of this whole work.

The Exodus

The YMCA progressed eastward with the Czechoslovaks as the line was opened in the fall of 1918. The Allies were in Central Siberia in 1919, but in the spring of that year there was much sharp fighting along the line.

Some vivid glimpses of the work in Irkutsk in 1919 are typical of the service in this period:

> Recently the great body of the Czechoslovak Army has been concentrated in Western Siberia between Irkutsk and Omsk, and it is in this section that the Y has put forth its greatest efforts. At Irkutsk nearly the entire First Division has been concentrated as well as the General Staff and Government Offices, and for the past three months the Czech work has been directed from that point. A large hall in the center of the city has been used in conjunction with the Czech Cultural Committee for lectures, concerts, plays, and cinema, while adjoining, the Y operated a small but attractive coffee house for the men. An orchestra of German prisoners of war, all professional musicians, was engaged for the various points about the city, and their concerts were especially appreciated by the patients in the large Czech hospital there.
>
> At Irkutsk also a most successful beginning was made this spring and summer at distinctly religious work. The ground had been prepared previously by Mr. Miller in a series of lectures, delivered to practically all the regiments, on the Association and its point of view, but it was a most pleasant surprise to have the direct religious work so heartily welcomed by the men, most of whom are out of sympathy with religious ideas and institutions, when not directly opposed to them....

Athletic work was much stimulated by the visit of the American doughboys to Irkutsk. The Americans came on for a three days' stay, and brought with them about 150 officers and men, including two baseball teams, one football team, exhibition boxers, and the 27th Infantry Band.

During the spring the Czechs who were stationed on the line between Irkutsk and Krasnoyarsk had a most busy time with their enemies who were doing their best to tear up the road, wreck trains, riddle them with bullets and generally make themselves disagreeable. It took three months to clear out their nest, and the Czechs had to go back over a hundred versts into the steppe after them. It was a most trying sort of work, as the men were mostly stationed at small stations and sidings absolutely cut off from the outside world and liable to be ambushed at any time by the Bolshevik bandits. Here our secretaries were indeed a friend in need. Our traveling cinema cars also rendered an enormous service to the men of this region as well as to those further on. The secretaries were instructed to stop at every station, no matter if there were no more than a dozen soldiers there, and stay at least a day and where possible two or three days, to mix with the men in the day time, get them playing football or volley ball, and in the evening to have the cinema performance in the open air.

Reviewing our work with the Czechs as a whole, one can of course see mistakes, failures, shortcomings. But taken all in all we have reason to believe that the Association has made good with the Czechs. Certainly they have been most appreciative of our feeble attempts to render them service commensurate to the service they have rendered the world by their deeds here in Siberia. The Association has no better friend in Siberia today than the Czechoslovak soldier, and let us hope that that friendship will continue long after he has stopped soldiering, and stay by him in the early days of his new Republic.

Work in Vladivostok

Four thousand miles away at the very eastern gateway of Siberia the same kind of service for the Czechs was going on. The comparatively few Y secretaries who were in Vladivostok worked heroically and enthusiastically for these new allies. They were aided by several others recalled from China and Japan where they were on their way home. After their previous disappointments in European Russia they found spring and summer in Vladivostok with the Czechs a most exhilarating and soul-satisfying experience. They had the sensation of being partners in romantic and heroic events and received a very ready response from the Czechs who always spoke of them by the familiar and affectionate term of "Strychek" (uncle).

The immediate problem in May and June, 1918, when it was assumed that the Czechs were on their way to France, was to make their long wait for transportation as bearable as possible and keep their spirits high. To this end the well-known Y recreational activities were employed. Movies were given outdoors, the men sitting by thousands on the hillsides. There were outdoor pavilions. The artistic instinct of the Czechs was utilized in landscape gardening about their barracks and clubs and interior decorations.

Every evening at sundown the troops would gather on a high promontory overlooking the magnificent harbor of Vladivostok, "the Queen of the East," and sing with ringing voices and deep emotion their national anthem, formerly forbidden in Austria: "Where is my home, Where is my home?"

By the end of June, ten barracks clubs were in operation and Y secretaries were ably assisting the officers in the difficult problems of preserving the morale and discipline of the troops from the demoralizing influence of an Oriental city. The soldiers became restless when they discovered that they were not going to France immediately. That the army was able to preserve a high state of morale through all this, with an astonishingly low venereal record, speaks volumes for the natural restraint and character of the Czechs as well as for the effectiveness of the program provided by the Association. One of the frequent comments of the soldiers at the clubs and movie shows was—"Now there is no need of going to the city."

This peaceful period suddenly came to a close. As already narrated, conflict with the Bolsheviks broke out. The spirit of the Czechs changed at once. They wanted to go back and help their brothers. Relations with the Soviet became strained, and on Saturday, June 29, 1918, the Czechs attacked and captured the city. The Y secretaries saw at once that barracks work was ended and that they must follow the Czechs on cars—if at all. Eight cars were placed on a siding for the use of the workers. On Monday, carpenters fitted them up and on Tuesday the first Y club car left for the West. By the end of the week four more were in operation.

Manufacturing Activities

Only a few days later, a train came back bearing 200 wounded Czechs. There were no Red Cross representatives in Siberia at that time, so the Y advanced the necessary funds to meet the needs of the wounded. Immediately there was a demand for canteen work at the front and the business turnover increased from 12,000 rubles in June to 2,000,000 in October, 1918. This service necessitated increased transportation facilities and imposed labor beyond the resources of the few secretaries available. Czech invalids were pressed into the supply service. With great difficulty, by taking over a biscuit factory and the increased production of several chocolate factories as well as by recourse to the markets of China, Japan, Korea and the Philippines, supplies were obtained. On the Ussuri Front north of Vladivostok, where the Czechs were fighting, the Y provided weekly on an average over 10,000 loaves of bread, two tons of chocolate, 10 tons of biscuits, and 1,000,000 cigarettes.

In the meantime there had been an enormous territorial expansion in the work. The first front had been only a few hundred miles north of Vladivostok. Now Y cars were running out a thousand miles across Manchuria. This fact created a new problem of supply. The American railroad engineers were able to aid in its solution, and by September the line was opened beyond Irkutsk into Western Siberia. New recruits began to arrive for the work, but not before several secretaries, who had been working at top speed night and day all summer, broke down under the strain. The first supply train got through to the Urals about the middle of September. By that time Allied forces had arrived in large numbers and the Y had the added responsibility of American and Allied troops.

Evacuation

The work of late 1919, and all of 1920, falls into three divisions, war prisoners' work, city work, and service with the Allied Armies. Some time after the Armistice, work with war prisoners in Siberia was resumed by the Y; and after the greater part of the American Allied forces were evacuated, these Germans, Austrians, Turks and others were cared for at the International Hut in Vladivostok. Supplies were furnished for their voyage to their homes, and secretaries accompanied some of them. The city work, reduced by 1920 to Vladivostok and Harbin, continued along the same lines followed for several years, but increased in membership and effectiveness. The great work of this period was that of the Army and Navy department.

For the first time in the history of Y work in Siberia conditions were favorable to really effective work. In the earlier period troops had been scattered in echelons over four or five thousand miles of railway track. Now they were being concentrated in large numbers in and around Vladivostok, and although it was a constantly changing body, the Y work remained the same until the Allied military population of Vladivostok faded away across the seas.

The International Hut at Vladivostok

The character of this work is best typified by the International Hut at Vladivostok, centrally located and open continuously to soldiers representing some ten or fifteen national armies. The Hut itself was spacious and compared very favorably with the biggest and best in France or England. The huge open fire did not go out once between October and May, 1919–20. There were daily music, movies, buffet and canteen service and a special program every evening, staged by one of the many nationalities served, or by some special entertainers. Athletic contests played a large part in these programs and educational work was carried on continually. A very conservative record shows that some 700,000 persons enjoyed the facilities of this Hut during eight months of 1920, which would indicate that in the entire period of its activity, it served over 1,000,000. This does not mean a million distinct individuals, as there were never more than a few hundred thousand soldiers of all nationalities put together in Siberia at that time. On the other hand, it means that many a soldier made a visit to the Hut every day and enjoyed its warmth and hospitality and the spirit of friendliness that permeated it. In the whole history of the International Hut there is no record of the slightest disorder among the various nationalities, many of them unfriendly and all armed. They left their national hatreds and animosities outside. Had the International Hut done nothing else but stand for the ideal of international brotherhood it would have justified its existence. How much more it accomplished in giving comfort of body and mind to tens of thousands of patient and war weary soldiers and prisoners of war cannot be measured.

Successful Repatriation Activities

The Y was able, thanks to adequate supplies and personnel, to provide a secretary with necessary equipment of all kinds, including cigarettes and chocolate for free distribution for each transport leaving Vladivostok. The evacuation of the AEF began in January and ended in April. The 67,217 Czechoslovaks were not finally evacuated until September, 1920, and in January, 1921, 2,000 Romanians and other small scattered units and war prisoners were still there.

It is a pleasure to record that after so many difficulties and discouragements the Y ended its Army work in Siberia on a full tide of success and won the sincere esteem of the many nationalities which it served.

Conclusion

At the moment of America's entry into the war, Allied hopes of Russia were high. The anomaly of an autocratic imperialism among the democratic Allied nations had been removed by the revolution. Russian soldiers had shown fighting characteristics warranting belief that their defeats were due more to treachery and intrigue in their own Government than to the superiority of their opponents. Relieved of the bureaucratic incubus, it was expected that the long suppressed but never quiescent spirit of liberty in the Russian people would make them a valuable factor in the Allied ranks. Although these hopes were disappointed, there was no question at the time as to the wisdom and importance of efforts to secure their fulfillment. Their direct bearing on American interests, clearly foreseen, was confirmed by events.

The Russian problem was but one of many with which the National War Work Council was struggling. In spite of the feeling of isolation and even of neglect which sometimes affected secretaries working in Russia, earnest thought and effort were, in America, continually devoted to their support. Nearly $8,000,000 were spent. The fortunes of war and rapidly changing political conditions were responsible for the lessened amounts that, in the form of supplies, reached their destination in the lives of soldiers. At one time and another the services of 442 men were furnished.

The direct results have been indicated—they cannot be measured—in the preceding pages. All the influences brought to bear by the Allied nations failed to keep Russia in the war. Probably the task was an impossible one. Successful Y service was rendered, in North Russia and Siberia, to some hundreds of thousands of soldiers of a dozen nations, including our own. Most striking were the services to the Czechoslovaks, whose profound gratitude was won, and that to evacuating troops in Eastern Siberia. Relief work, in cooperation with and at times substitution for the American Red Cross, was done for civilians and refugees.

A Future Harvest

Of this work the results are still to be harvested. The world cannot remain in the chaos of recent years. It must return to the ways of peace. Seeds of opportunity for permanent civilian work have been planted. The soldiers whom the Association especially sought to serve will constitute a major part of the citizenship of the Russia which is to be. The millions of civilians ministered to by the Y and the Red Cross have learned the reality of American sympathy.

When the day of Russian reconstruction for which the whole world anxiously looks shall arrive, with its need of every possible character and morale building agency, the stock of goodwill accumulated through Association service to the Russian people will open wide opportunities for American helpfulness.

INDEX

Alexandrov, Vladimir V., 17, 17n29, 21
Allied intervention, xv, xvi, 67, 68
Anderson, Paul B., xviii, xix
Andrew, Bishop (Ukhtomsky), 18, 18n30
Archangelsk, xvi, 55, 67, 69, 71, 72

Baseball, 58
Beliaev, Mikhail Alekseevich, xiii
Berlin, xviii, 41
Bertron, Samuel R., 14, 14n21
Bolsheviks, xix, 53, 59, 60, 74, 87
British and Foreign Bible Society, 23, 23n42

Cathedral of Christ the Savior, 19, 19n34
Catholics, Roman, xiii, xx, 16, 24, 50, 51
classes, 47, 57
Colton, Ethan, xiv, 61, 64
Council, Russian Church, 16, 16n26, 18
Crane, Charles R., 14, 14n19, 17, 19, 25, 27
Czechoslovaks, 53, 54, 55, 65, 68, 75, 76, 77, 80, 82, 83, 84, 85, 86, 87, 89, 90

Davis, Jerome, xiii, xiv, xvii, xix, 61
Day, George, xiii
Duncan, James, 14, 14n22

Eddy, Sherwood, xix

Faith and Order Movement, 30, 30n48
February Revolution, ix, xix, 4, 4n3, 15, 24, 25, 54
Francis, David R., 8, 8n12

Gaylord, Franklin A., 56
Glennon, James H., 14, 14n18

Harbin, 67, 77, 78
Harte, Archibald, xiii, xiv, 6, 41, 44, 52, 61, 62, 63
Hecker, Julius, xix

Holy Synod, 15, 16, 17, 18, 21, 22
Irkutsk, xiii, 5, 45, 52, 59, 78

Jews, xiii, xx, 15, 24, 50, 51, 65, 81

Kazan, xiii, 57, 60
Kazan Cathedral, 21, 21n40, 59
Keen, William, 23, 23n42
Kerensky, Alexander F., xvii, 5, 5n9, 59, 62
Khabarovsk, 78
Kiev, xiii, 42, 60
kitchens, 49, 50
Kolchak, Alexander V., 80, 80n18, 82
Kropotkin, Peter A., 6, 6n10
Kuropatkin, Aleksei Nikolaevich, xiii, 56

Lenin, Vladimir, xvii, xviii
libraries, 47
Lowrie, Donald A., xiii
Lubianka prison, xviii
Lubimov, Nikolai A., 20, 20n38
Lvov, Georgy E., Prince, 5, 5n7, 59
Lvov, Vladimir N., 15n24, 31, 31n49

Mayak, ix, 8, 8n13, 9, 56, 57, 62, 78
McCormick, Cyrus H., Jr., 14, 14n20
Methodist Episcopal Church, 24, 24n43
Minsk, 59
Moscow, xiii, xvi, xvii, 9, 15, 19, 42, 47, 53, 59, 62, 63, 66
Mott, John R., ix, xi, xii, xiv, xvii, xviii, xix, 3, 8, 12, 14, 25, 30, 31, 42, 54, 64
Murmansk, xvi, 55, 67, 69, 71, 72
music, 48
Muslims (Mohammedans), 50, 51

Nicholas II, Emperor, xiv, xv, xviii
Nikolai, Archbishop (Kasatkin), 26, 26n46
Nobel, Emanuel L., 8, 8n11
Novo-Nikolaevsk (Novosibirsk), 78

Ober-Procurator (high procurator), 15, 15n24, 18, 19, 23, 24, 30, 31, 42
October Revolution, xiv, xv, xviii, xix, 53, 54, 63
Odessa, xiii, 59
Old Believers, 16, 16n27, 18, 23
Omsk, xiii, 47, 58, 80, 81
Orenburg, 47, 51, 57

Paris, xviii
Pershing, John J., 12, 12n17, 28
Petrograd, xv, xvii, xviii, 5, 5n5, 8, 9, 10, 14, 15, 18, 21, 30, 41, 42, 47, 51, 52, 53, 56, 57, 59, 62, 78
Platon, Archbishop (Rozhdestvensky), 17, 17n28, 18, 21, 27
Pobedonostsev, Konstantin, 19, 19n32
prisoners (POWs), x, xi, xii, xiii, xiv, xv, xvii, xx, 3, 5, 7, 20, 22, 26, 27, 41, 43, 44, 46, 47, 48, 49, 51, 52, 53, 54, 55, 57, 58, 64, 67, 82, 85, 89
Protestants, xiii, xx, 16, 18, 20, 24, 50
Provisional Government, ix, xv, 7, 22, 29, 54, 59

Rasputin, Grigory, 15, 15n25
Root, Elihu, ix, xv, xviii, 4, 4n2, 14, 25, 54
Russell, Charles Edward, 14, 14n23
Russian Civil War, xv
Russian Orthodox Church, ix, xii, xv, 15, 17, 18, 19, 20, 23, 24, 25, 26, 27, 28, 30, 31, 77, 79

Samara, xv, 55, 61, 64, 67, 77
Samarin, Alexander D., 20, 20n37
Scott, Hugh L., 12, 12n16, 13, 14
Simons, George A., 24, 24n43
socialism, xviii, xix

soldiers, x, xii, xiii, xiv, xv, xvi, xvii, xviii, xx, 3, 4, 4n4, 5, 6, 10, 11, 43, 48, 53, 55, 57, 58, 59, 60, 61, 62, 63, 71, 74, 75, 76, 77, 85, 88, 89, 90
Stevens, John Frank, 21, 21n41
Stokes, James, 56

Tashkent, 5
Tereshchenko, Mikhail I., 5, 5n8, 59
Tikhon, Archbishop (Metropolitan, Patriarch) (Bellavin), 20, 20n36, 27, 66
Tomsk, xiii, 5, 47, 57, 78
Treaty of Brest-Litovsk, xiv, xv, 53, 59
Trotsky, Leon, xvii, xviii
Trubetskoy, Evgeny N., 18, 18n31
Turkestan, xiii, xvii, 5, 5n6, 43, 56

Uspensky Cathedral, 20, 20n39

Verkhovsky, Alexander I., 62, 62n13
Vladivostok, xvi, 9, 42, 55, 67, 68, 75, 77, 84, 86, 87, 88, 89
Volga Agricultural Expedition, 66

Wheeler, Crawford, 61, 71
Wilson, Woodrow, ix, xi, xii, xiii, xvii, 4, 4n1, 8, 10, 14, 17, 22, 25, 64, 81
workshops, 48
World War I, ix, xx

Young Men's Christian Association (Association, YMCA, Y), ix, x, xi, xii, xiii, xiv, xv, xvi, xvii, xix, xx, 4, 5, 6, 8n13, 9, 10, 11, 12, 42, 44, 45, 46, 48, 51, 54, 55, 56, 58, 59, 60, 61, 62, 63, 64, 66, 67, 68, 69, 70, 71, 72, 73, 74, 75, 76, 77, 78, 79, 81, 82, 83, 84, 85, 86, 87, 88, 89, 90

www.ingramcontent.com/pod-product-compliance
Lightning Source LLC
Chambersburg PA
CBHW032029230426
43671CB00005B/251